AN ABRIDGMENT OF
THE ARCHITECTURE OF VITRUVIUS

LECTOR HOUSE PUBLIC DOMAIN WORKS

AN ABRIDGMENT OF THE ARCHITECTURE OF VITRUVIUS

VITRUVIUS, CLAUDE PERRAULT

ISBN: 978-93-89679-62-5

Published: 1692

LECTOR HOUSE LLP
E-MAIL: lectorpublishing@gmail.com

ARCHITECTURE, 1692.

AN ABRIDGMENT OF
THE ARCHITECTURE OF VITRUVIUS.

CONTAINING A SYSTEM OF THE WHOLE WORKS OF THAT AUTHOR.

ILLUSTRATED WITH DIVERS COPPER PLATES, CURIOUSLY ENGRAVED; WITH A TABLE OF EXPLANATION,

To which is added in this Edition
The Etymology and Derivation of the Terms used in Architecture.

First done in French by Monsr Perrault, of the Academy of Paris, and now Englished, with Additions.

1692.

TO THE READER.

Abridgments of Vitruvius *have been formerly printed, but none of them have followed the design which* Philebert de l'Orme *has given in his Third Book: He desires that in abridging* Vitruvius *the matters which this Author treats of confusedly should be put into order, and that the things belonging to the same Subject, which are found dispersed in divers places, should be collected together into one Chapter. This Method, which the most part of the eminent Writers have neglected, has been carefully observed in this Treatise, it serving very much to the better apprehending and retaining the things treated of. We have been exact to put in nothing that is not taken out of* Vitruvius, *to which end the* Book *and* Chapter *of his Works are all along quoted in the Margin; nothing being added, but some few lines here and there, to continue the Discourse, and render it more clear: Notwithstanding which precautions, some things may possibly still remain obscure, in which case the Reader must have Recourse to the whole Works of* Vitruvius, *where he will find all necessary Explanation.*

This little Treatise is not only necessary for those who begin the study of Architecture, but will be also of great use to even Masters themselves; for it is not to be doubted, that Vitruvius *being so great a Master in this Art, his Authority, together with that of all the Ancients, which is included in his Works, must be capable of instructing the Apprentices, and confirming the Masters, and thereby establish the good Maxims and certain Rules of Architecture.*

ADVERTISEMENT CONCERNING THIS TRANSLATION.

This Abridgment having been very well received in French, we have ventured to put it in English, and doubt not but it will be as acceptable to our Nation, who are allowed to be as competent Judges of this Art as any. The Translation is very exact; the Cutts altogether as well, if not better, than in the French; and in the Table of the Explication of the Terms used in Architecture, we have added the Etymology and Derivation of them, which is not in the French.

CONTENTS

CHAP. IV.

OF THE BEAUTY OF BUILDINGS.

PART II.
CONTAINING THE ARCHITECTURE PECULIAR TO THE ANCIENTS.

CHAP. I.

OF PUBLICK BUILDINGS.

In Fortification four things are consider'd; the disposition of the Ramparts; the Figure of the whole place, the building of the Walls; thickness, materials, and terrass; the figure and disposition of the

CHAP. II.

OF PRIVATE BUILDINGS.

CHAP. III.

OF THINGS THAT EQUALLY APPERTAIN TO PUBLICK AND PRIVATE BUILDINGS.

AN ABRIDGMENT OF THE TEN BOOKS OF THE ARCHITECTURE OF VITRUVIUS.

THE INTRODUCTION.

ARTICLE I.

Of the great Merits of Vitruvius, and the Excellencies of his Works.

There are so many things in the Works of *Vitruvius* that do not directly appertain to Architecture, that one would think they were less fitted to Instruct those that have a design to learn the Precepts of this Art, than to perswade the World that the Author was the most knowing Architect that ever was, and a Person of the greatest Merit: He had the Honour to serve *Julius Cæsar* and *Augustus*, the two Greatest and most Magnificent Princes of the World, in an Age when all things were come to the highest degree of Perfection.

Lib. 6. Preface.

For one may see in reading his Works, which are full of a wonderful variety of Matters, which he treats of with a singular Erudition, that this great Man had acquired that Profound Knowledge which is necessary for his Profession by more excellent Methods, and more capable of producing something excellent, than the bare exercise and ordinary practice of a Mechanical Art could possibly do; being compleat in all the Liberal Arts and Sciences, and his great Wit being accustomed, even from his Cradle, to understand the most difficult Matters: He had acquired a certain Facility which meer Artizans have not, of penetrating the deepest Secrets, and all the difficulties of so vast an Art, as that of Architecture.

Lib. 2. Pref.

Lib. 6. Preface.

Now as it's true that in the Practice and Exercise of Arts, one does not always easily distinguish the Abilities of those that work in them. The great Capacity of *Vitruvius* before the publishing of his Book, which he Composed when he was in Years, had not all the Esteem it deserved; which he complains of in his Preface, and in the Age he lived; though it was full of the most refined Wits, yet he had the fortune of others, to find few to defend him from the Surprizes and Attacks of false Reasoning, and from the injustice that prejudice creates, to those who apply themselves more to cultivate the Talents they possess, than to make parade of them.

Lib. 2. Pref.

Lib. 6. Pref.

Lib. 3. Pref.

Lib. 3. Pref.

Lib. 6. Pref.

Vitruvius was a Man, who, as to the exteriour, made a small Figure, and who had not heaped up great Riches by the practice of his Profession; and having, as it were, buried himself in study, and wholly given himself over to the Contemplation of Sciences, understood little of the Arts of the Court, or the Crafty Slights of pushing on his Fortune and making himself considerable; for though he was bestowed upon, and recommended to *Augustus*, by the Princess *Octavia* his Sister, we cannot find that he was employed in any Works of great Importance. The Noblest Edifice that we can learn that *Augustus* caused to be built, was, the Theatre of *Marcellus*; and this was done by another Architect: And the only Fabrick we can find he was employed in was not at *Rome*, but at *Fano*, a very little City; insomuch, that the greatest part of the Architects of that Age, who had gained the general Vogue, being so ignorant, that they did not know even (as himself is forced to declare) the first Principles of their Art: The Quality of a mere Architect was become so Contemptible, that if his Books had not carried all the Marks of an extraordinary Knowledge, and rare abilities, and undeceived the World by taking away the prejudice that his small employ created him, the Precepts he has left us would have wanted that Authority that was necessary to support them.

For Architecture being an Art that has scarce any other Rule to walk by, in performing all those Excellencies her Works are capable of, than what we call a Good Fancy, which truly distinguishes that which is Beautiful and Good from that which is not so; it's absolutely necessary that one be perswaded that the Fancy he follows is better than any other; to the end, that this Perswasion insinuating it self into them that study this Art, it may form in them a Correct and Regular Idea, which without this Perswasion, would be always floating and uncertain; so that to establish this Good Fancy, it's necessary to have one to whom we give great deference, and who has merited great Credit by the Learning that is found in his Writings; and is believed to have had sufficient abilities of chusing well among all Antiquity, that which is most solid and capable of founding the Precepts of Architecture.

The Veneration we have for the first Inventers of Arts, is not only Natural, but it's founded upon Reason; which makes us judge, that he that had the first Thought, and first invented any Thing, must needs have had a fitter Genius, and a better Capacity for it, than all those that afterwards laboured to bring it to its utmost Perfection. The *Greeks*, who were the Inventers of Architecture, as well as of other Sciences, having left many Works behind them as well in Building as in Books, which were looked upon in the time of *Vitruvius*, as the Models of what was perfect and accomplished in this Art, *Vitruvius* chiefly followed and imitated them; and in the Composition of his Book, gathered from them all that was to be found Excellent and Rare in all their Works; which makes us believe, that he has omitted nothing that was necessary, to form the General Idea of Good and Beautiful, since there is not the least probability that any thing could escape so Rare a Wit, Illuminated with so many different Lights.

But because at present the Reputation of *Vitruvius* is so generally established, that all Ages have placed him in the first Rank of great Wits, and that there is nothing necessary to recommend the Precepts of Architecture, but to prove they were drawn out of his Works: We having here designed to make only an Abridgment of his Works, we thought it would be necessary to cut off many things that this Famous Author has drawn out of an infinity of Writers, whose Works are now lost, and only gives a short Account of the Contents of every Book, in the beginning of this Abridgment; handling only in this Book, those Things that directly belong to Architecture; disposing the Matter in a different Method from that of *Vitruvius*, who often leaves off the Matter he is treating of, and takes it up again in another place.

The Order we have proposed to our selves in this Abstract, is, That after having given an Account in few words of what is contained in the whole Book; we Explain more particularly what we judge may be serviceable to those that study Architecture. This Treatise is divided into Two Parts; The First contains the Maxims and Precepts that may be accommodated to *Modern* Architecture; the Second contains all that appertains to the *Ancient* and *Antique* Architectures; which, though often affected, have little that's now made use of, may yet nevertheless serve to form the Judgment, and regulate the Fancy, and serve for Examples of things that may be useful.

I make a Distinction between the *Ancient* Architecture, and the *Antique* Architecture, and the *Modern*; for we call that Architecture *Ancient* of which *Vitruvius* has writ, and of which we may as yet see many Examples in the Fabricks that remain in *Greece*. The Architecture which we call *Antique*, is that which may be found in the Famous Edifices, which, since the Time of *Vitruvius*, were built at *Rome*, *Constantinople*, and many other places. The *Modern*, is that which being more accommodated to the present use, or for other Reasons, has changed some of the Dispositions and Proportions which were observed by the *Ancient* and *Antique* Architects.

ARTICLE II.

The Method of the Works of Vitruvius, with short Arguments of every Book.

Lib. 1.Chap. 3.

All his Works are divided into Three Parts: The First Treats of Building; The Second is Gnomonical, and treats at large of Astronomical and Geometrical Affairs. The Third gives Rules and Examples for making Machines or Engines serviceable, either in War or Building. The First Part is treated of in the Eight first Books: The Second in the Ninth: The Third in the Last.

The First Part which relates to Building is twofold, for they are either publick or private. He speaks of private Buildings in the Sixth Book; and as to that which relates to publick Buildings, it's likewise divided into Three Parts, *viz.* That which has Relation to Security, which consists in Fortifications, described in the Third Chapter of the First Book; That which appertains to Religion, of which he treats in the Third and Fourth Books, and that which relates to publick Conveniencies, as *Town-Houses, Theatres, Baths, Academies, Market-places, Gates*; of which he treats in the Fifth Book.

> *A division of his whole Works into three parts, whereof 1. treats of Building, 2. Gnomonical, 3. Mechanical. A second division into three parts, 1. of Solidity, 2. of Convenience, and 3. of Beauty. The Arguments of the Ten Books.*

The Gnomonical part is treated of in the Ninth Book.

The Third Part which treats of Machines, is treated of in the Tenth and Last Book.

Besides these particular Matters of Architecture, there are Three things that appertain to all sort of Edifices, which are, Solidity, Convenience, and Beauty. He speaks of Solidity in the Eleventh Chapter of the Sixth Book; of Convenience, in the Seventh Chapter of the same Book; and of Beauty through the whole Chapter of the Seventh Book; which contains all the Ornaments that Painting and Sculpture are capable of giving to all sorts of Fabricks; and as to Proportion, which ought to be esteemed one of the principal Foundations of Beauty, it's treated of throughout all his Works.

But to make it better understood, in what Method every Book explains those things, we must tell you, That in the First Book, after having treated of those things that belong to Architecture in General, by the Enumeration of the Parts that compose it, and of those that are required in an Architect, the Author explains in particular what choice ought to be made of the Seat where we ought to Build, as to Health and Convenience; after he speaks of the Foundations and of the Building of Fortifications, and the Form of Towers and Walls of Cities, he dilates himself upon the Air and Healthiness of the Situation.

In the Second Book, he speaks of the Original of Architecture, and what were the first Habitations of Mankind; after he treats of the Materials, *viz.* of Brick, Sand, Lime, Stones, and Timber: After which he treats of the different Methods of laying, binding, and Masonry of Stones. He Philosophizes upon their Principles, and upon the Nature of Lime, upon the choice of Sand, and the time of cutting of Wood.

The Third Book treats of the Proportion of the Temples, and of seven sorts of them which are those called *Antes, Prostyle, Amphiprostyle, Periptere, Pseudiptere, Diptere* and *Hypæthre*. After he speaks of the Different spaces that ought to be betwxit every Pillar, to which he gives the Five Names following, (which in the latter Part of this Book shall be more fully explained, as well as divers Terms of Art) *viz. Pycnostyle, Systyle, Diastyle, Aræostyle* and *Eustyle*. After that, he gives in particular the Proportions of the *Ionick* Order, and demonstrates that it has a Proportion with Humane Bodies.

The Fourth gives the Proportion of the *Corinthian* and *Dorick* Orders for Temples, with the Proportions of all the Parts that compose them.

The Fifth treats of Publick Fabricks, *viz.* of *Market-places, Theatres, Palaces, Baths, Schools* for Sciences, and *Academies* for Exercises, and in Conclusion, of *Sea-Ports*; and after occasionally discourses at large upon Musick, because, speaking of Theatres, he gives an account how the Ancient Architects, were in some places of the Theatre wont to place Vessels of Brass to serve for several sorts of tunable Echo's, and augmenting the Voice of the Comedians.

In the Sixth he teaches what were the Proportions and Forms of private Houses among the Greeks and Romans, as well in the City as Country; and describes all the parts of the House, *viz.* the Courts, Porches, Halls, Dining Rooms, Chambers, Cabinets and Libraries.

In the Seventh he treats of the manner of making use of Mortar for Plaster and Floors; how Lime and the Powder of Marble ought to be prepared to make Stuck. He speaks likewise of the Ornaments that are common to all sorts of Buildings, as Painting; and all sorts of Colours, as well Natural as Artificial, that the Ancients made use of.

In the Eighth he speaks of Waters, and Rivers, and Fountains; *viz.* of their Springs, of their Nature, and Properties; how they are to be sought; and of the Conduits that are to bring them to Cities and Villages.

The Ninth is wholly Gnomonical, and teaches the manner of making Sun-Dials, and gives an account of the Rules of Geometry, how to measure solid Bodies. He discourses at large of the Course of the Stars, and the particular Description of those that are called Fixed Stars.

The Last is taken up wholly in the Description of making Machines to lift up great Weights, and others for several uses; *viz.* for the Elevation of Water for Corn-Mills, Water-Organs and Measuring the Way as well by Sea as by Land; but it chiefly treats of Machines fit for the use of Building and War.

PART I.
OF ARCHITECTURE THAT IS COMMON TO US WITH THE ANCIENTS.

CHAP. 1.

OF ARCHITECTURE IN GENERAL.

ARTICLE I.

Of the Original of Architecture.

The first occasion of Architecture; the Models of the first Architects. The Inventers of the four Orders of Architecture.

Lib. 2. Chap. 1.

Lib. 4. Chap. 2.

It's related by Historians, That Men, who in former times inhabited Woods and Caverns like wild Beasts, first assembled themselves to make Houses and Cities, which was occasioned by a Forest that was set on fire, which drew all the Inhabitants together by its novelty and surprizing effects; so that many Men meeting together in the same place, they found out means, by helping one another, to harbour themselves more conveniently, than in Caves and under Trees; so that it is pretended, that Architecture was the Beginning and Original of all other Arts. For Men seeing that they had success in Building, which necessity made them invent, they had the Thoughts and Courage of seeking out other Arts, and applying themselves to them.

Now even as they took Trees, Rocks and other Things that Nature her self furnished Beasts to harbour themselves under, which were made use of as Models for the first Houses, which at first were only made of green Turf and broken Branches of Trees, they made use of them afterwards, in the same manner, to arrive at something more perfect. For passing from the Imitation of the Natural to that of Artificial, they invented all the Ornaments of Edifices that were most curiously wrought, in giving them the Form and Shape of those things that are simply necessary to the most natural Buildings: And the Pieces of Timber of which the Roofs and Floors of Houses are made, were the Original of *Pillars, Architraves, Frises, Triglyphs, Mutils, Brackets, Corniches, Frontons* or *Piediments,* which are made of Stone or Marble.

The Pillars which are to be smaller at top than at bottom, were made in Imitation of the Boles or Trunks of Trees, and their use was taken from the Carpenters' Posts that are made to support the Building. The *Architraves* which are laid across many *Pillars,* represent *Summers* that join many *Posts* together. The *Frises* imitate the *Muring* that is raised upon the *Summers* betwixt the ends of the Beams that are laid directly upon the *Pillars*. The *Triglyphs* represent the Ceiling or Joyner's work which was made upon the ends of the Beams to conserve them. The *Corniches* are as it were the extream parts of the *Joists*. The *Modillions* represent the ends of the Sheers, and the *Dentels* represent the ends of the principal *Rafter*. The *Frontons* are made in imitation of the *Firms* or *Girders*, upon which is laid the Roof of the House.

Lib. 4. Chap. 2.

There is likewise another Original of Architecture, which is taken from the Inventers of the several Orders, and those that added the Ornaments to embellish them. For it's the common Opinion, that the first Fabrick that was made, according to any of the Orders, was the Temple that King *Dorus* built in Honour of *Juno* in the City *Argos*. And it obtained the name of the *Dorick* Order, when *Ion* the Conducter of a Colony, which he established in *Asia*, made many Temples be built according to the Model of the Temple built by *Dorus* in *Greece*.

But the *Ionians* having changed some of the Proportions and Ornaments of the *Dorick* Order, were the Authors of another Order, which was called the *Ionick*, according to which, they built a Temple in Honour of *Diana*. The reason of this change was, that this Temple being dedicated to a Divinity, which they represented under the Shape of a Young Lady, they thought it was proper to make their Pillars more tapering, the better to represent the airy Stature of this Goddess, and for this reason they adorned it more delicately, adding Bases which represent the Buskin'd Ornaments of the Legs and Feet, according to the Mode of that time; and Made the *Channellings* deeper to represent the Foldings and Plaits of a fine light Garment. They put likewise *Volutes* or *Scrowls* upon the *Capital*, pretending that they imitated the Head-Dress of a Young Lady, whose Hair Beautifully descending from the top of her Head, was folded up under each Ear.

Afterwards *Calimachus* an *Athenian*, embellished the Capitals of the Pillars, adding to them more Beautiful *Volutes* or *Scrowls*, and more in number, enriching them with the Leaves of *Brank Ursine* and Roses. It's said, That this Capital, which, according to *Vitruvius*, makes all the Distinction betwixt the *Corinthian* and *Ionick* Order, was invented by this ingenious Artisan upon this occasion. Having seen the Leaves of the above-mentioned Plant grow round about a Basket which was set upon the Tomb of a Young *Corinthian* Lady, and which, as it happened, was set upon the middle of the Plant. He represented the Basket by the *Tambour* or *Vase* of the Capital, to which he made an *Abacus* to imitate the Tile with which the Basket was covered, and that he represented the Stalks of the Herb by the *Volutes* or *Scrowls*, which were ever after placed upon the *Corinthian* Capital. See Table the IXth.

This great Artist likewise invented other Ornaments, as those we call *Eggs*, because of the *Ovals* in the *Relief* which are in the Mouldings of the *Corniches* and are like *Eggs*. The Ancients called this Ornament *Echinus*, which signifies the sharp prickly shell of Chestnuts, because they found these Ovals represented a Chestnut half open, as it is when it's ripe.

Lib. 3. Chap. 2.

He likewise makes mention of another Famous Author, who found out the proportion of all the Parts of a Fabrick, which was *Hermogenes*; to whom he attributes the Invention of the *Eustyle, Pseudodiptere,* and of all that is beautiful and excellent in Architecture.

ARTICLE II.

What Architecture is.

Definition of it; an Architect ought to have the knowledge of eleven things, viz. Writing, Designing, Geometry, Arithmetick, History. Philosophy, moral and natural. Physick, Law, Astronomy, and Musick.

Lib. 1. Chap. 1.

Architecture is a Science which ought to be accompanied with the Knowledge of a great many other Arts and Sciences, by which means it forms a correct Judgment of all the Works of other Arts that appertain to it. This Science is acquired by *Theory* and *Practice.* The *Theory* of *Architecture* is that Knowledge of this Art which is acquired by study, travelling and discourse. The Practick is that knowledge that is acquired by the Actual Building of great Fabricks. These Two Parts are so necessary, that never any came to any great Perfection without them both. The one being lame and imperfect without the other, so they must walk hand in hand.

Besides, the Knowledge of things that particularly belong to Architecture, there are infinite other things that are necessary to be known by an Architect.

For, First, it's necessary that he be able to couch in writing his intended Building, and to design the Plan, and make an excellent Model of it.

Geometry likewise is very necessary for him in many occasions.

He must also know Arithmetick to make a true Calculation.

He must be knowing in History, and be able to give a reason for the greatest part of the Ornaments of Architecture which are founded upon History. For Example, if instead of Pillars he support the Floors of the House with the figures of Women, which are called *Cariatides,* he ought to know that the *Greeks* invented these Figures to let Posterity know the Victories they obtained over the *Cariens,* whose Wives they made Captives, and put their Images in their Buildings.

It's necessary likewise, that he be instructed in the Precepts of Moral Philosophy; for he ought to have a great Soul, and be bold without Arrogance, just, faithful, and totally exempt from Avarice.

Lib. 1. Chap. 11.

The Architect also ought to have a great Docility which may hinder him from neglecting the advice that is given him, not only by the meanest Artist, but also by those that understand nothing of Architecture; for not only Architects, but all the

World must judge of his Works.

Lib. 1. Chap. 2.

Natural Philosophy is likewise necessary for him for to discover what are the Causes of many things which he must put a remedy to.

He ought also to know something of *Physick*, to know the qualities of the Air, which makes Places Healthful and Habitable, or the quite contrary.

He should not be ignorant of the Laws and the Customs of Places for the Building of Partition Walls, for prospect and for the conveying of Waters and Sewers.

He ought to know *Astronomy*, that he may be able to make all sorts of Dials.

It was necessary among the Ancients, that an Architect should have skill in *Musick* to make and order *Catapults* and other Machines of War, which were strung with strings made of Guts, whose sound they were to observe, that they might judge of the strength and stiffness of the Beams which were bended with those Strings. *Musick* was also necessary in those days for the placing musically Vessels of Brass in the Theatres, as we have said before.

ARTICLE III.

What are the Parts of Architecture.

There are eight parts in Architecture, viz. 1. Solidity. 2. Convenience, 3. Beauty, 4. Order, 5. Disposition. 6. Proportion, 7. Decorum, 8. Oeconomy.

There are Three Things which ought to meet in every Fabrick, *viz. Solidity, Convenience* and *Beauty*, which Architecture gives them; by the due ordering and disposition of all the Parts that compose the Edifice, and which she rules by a just Proportion, having regard to a true *Decorum*, and well regulated *Oeconomy*; from whence it follows, that Architecture has Eight Parts, *viz. Solidity, Convenience, Beauty, Order, Disposition, Decorum, Oeconomy*.

Solidity depends upon the goodness of the Foundation, choice of Materials, and the right use of them; which ought to be with a due order, disposition and convenient Proportion of all Parts together, and of one in respect of another.

Convenience likewise consists in the ordering and disposition, which is so good that nothing hinders the use of any part of the Edifice.

Beauty consists in the excellent and agreeable form, and the just proportion of all its parts.

Order is that which makes, that all the parts of an Edifice have a convenient bigness, whether we consider them apart or with Relation to the whole.

Disposition is the orderly Ranging and agreeable Union of all the parts that compose the Work; so that as Order respects the Greatness, Disposition respects Form and Situation, which are Two Things compriz'd under the word *Quality*, which *Vitruvius* attributes to Disposition, and opposes to Quantity, which appertains to Order. There are three ways by which the Architect may take a view beforehand of the Fabrick he is to build, *viz.* First, *Ichnography*, which is the *Geometrical* Plan; *Orthography*, which is the *Geometrical Elevation*, and *Scenography*, which is *Perspective Elevation*.

Proportion, which is also call'd *Eurythmy*, is that which makes the Union of all parts of the Work, and which renders the Prospect agreeable, when the Height answers the Breadth, and the Breadth the Length; every one having its just measure. It is defin'd, the Relation that all the Work has with its Parts, and which every one of them has separately to the Idea of the whole, according to the measure of any Part. For as in Humane Bodies there is a Relation between the Foot, Hand, Finger and other Parts; so amongst Works that are Perfect, from any particular Part, we may make a certain Judgment of the Greatness of the whole Work: For Example, the Diameter of a Pillar, or the Length of a *Triglyph*, creates in us a right Judgment of the Greatness of the whole Temple.

And here we must remark, that to express the Relation that many things have one to another, as to their Greatness or different Number of Parts, *Vitruvius* indifferently makes use of three words, which are *Proportion, Eurythmy* and *Symmetry*. But we have thought it proper only to make use of the word Proportion, because *Eurythmy* is a Greek word, which signifies nothing else but Proportion; and Symmetry, although a word commonly used, does not signifie in the Vulgar Languages what *Vitruvius* understands by Proportion; for he understands by Proportion, a Relation according to Reason; and Symmetry, in the vulgar Languages, signifies only, a Relation of Parity and Equality. For the word *Simmetria* signifies in Latin and Greek *Relation* only. As for Example, as the Relation that Windows of Eight Foot high, have with other Windows of Six Foot, when the one are Four Foot broad, and the other Three: and Symmetry, in the Vulgar Languages, signifies the Relation, for Example, That Windows have one to another, when they are all of an equal height and equal breadth; and that their Number and Distances are equal to the Right and the Left; so that if the distances be unequal of one side, the like inequality is to be found in the other.

Decorum or Decency, is that which makes the Aspect of the Fabrick so correct, that there is nothing that is not approv'd of, and founded upon some Authority. It teaches us to have regard to three things, which are, *Design, Custom* and *Nature*.

The Regard to Design makes us chuse for Example, other Dispositions and Propertions for a Palace than for a Church.

The Respect we have to Custom, is the Reason, for Example, That the Porches and Entries of Houses are adorned, when the Inner Parts are Rich and Magnificent.

The Regard we have to the Nature of Places, makes us chuse different Prospects for different Parts of the Fabrick, to make them the wholsomer and the more convenient: For Example, the Bed-Chambers and the Libraries are exposed to the Morning Sun; the Winter Apartments, to the West; the Closets or Pictures and other Curiosities, which should always have equal Light, to the North.

Oeconomy teaches the Architect to have regard to the Expences that are to be made, and to the Quality of the Materials, near the Places where he Builds, and to take his Measures rightly for the Order and Disposition; *viz.* to give the Fabrick a convenient Form and Magnitude.

These Eight Parts, as we have said, have a Relation to the Three first, *viz. Solidity, Convenience, Beauty,* which suppose, *Order, Disposition, Proportion, Decorum* and *Oeconomy.* This is the reason that we divide this first Part only into Three Chapters; the first is of the Solidity; the second of the Convenience; the third of the Beauty of the Fabrick.

CHAP. II.

OF THE SOLIDITY OF BUILDINGS.

ARTICLE I.

Of the Choice of Materials.

Vitruvius speaks of five sorts of Materials, 1. Stone. 2. Bricks. 3. Wood, whereof divers sorts are used, as Oak, Fir, Poplar, Alder. Pine, Cypress, Juniper, Cedar, Larch and Olive; 4. Lime; 5. Sand and Gravel of which several sorts, Pit, River, and Pozzalane.

The Materials of which *Vitruvius* speaks are, Stone, Brick, Wood, Lime, and Sand.

All the Stones are not of one sort, for some are soft, some harder, and some extreamly hard.

Those that are not hard are easily cut, and are good for the Inner Parts of the Buildings, where they are cover'd from Rain and Frost which brings them to Powder, and if they be made use of in Buildings near the Sea, the Salt Particles of the Air and Heat destroys them.

Those that are indifferently hard, are fit to bear Weight; but there are some sorts of them, that easily crack with the heat of the Fire.

There is likewise another sort of Stone, which is a kind of Free-Stone; some are Red, some Black, and some White, which are as easily cut with a Saw as Wood.

The best Bricks are those which are only dry'd and not baked in the Fire; but there are many Years required to dry them well: and for this Reason, at *Utica*, a City of *Africa*, they made a Law, That none should make use of Bricks which had not been made five Years: For these sort of Bricks, so dry'd, had their Pores so close in their Superficies, that they would swim upon Water like a Pumice-Stone; and they had a particular Lightness, which made them very fit for all sorts of Buildings.

The Earth of which these Bricks were usually made was very Fat, and a sort of White Chalky Clay without Gravel or Sand, which made them Lighter and more Durable; they mixed Straw with them to make them better bound and firmer.

The Woods which were made use of in all Buildings, are Oak, Poplar, Beech, Elm, Cypress, Firr; but some of them are not so proper for Building as others.

The Firr, because it has great plenty of Air, and Fire, and but little Earth and

Water, is light, and does not easily bend; but is very subject to Worms and Fire.

The Oak which is more Earthy lasts for ever under Ground; but above Ground is apt to cleave.

The Beech which has little of Earthiness, Humidity and Fire, but great plenty of Air, is not very solid and easily breaks.

The Poplar and the Linden Trees are only good for light Work, they are easily cut and so finest for Carving.

The Alder is good to make Piles of in Marshy Places.

The Elm and the Ash have this property, that they do not easily cleave, and that they are pliable.

The Yoke-Elm is likewise pliable, and yet very strong; this is the Reason that they made Yokes for their Oxen of them in Old Time.

The Pine and the Cypress have this defect, that they easily bend under any Weight, because of their great Humidity; but they have this Advantage, that their Humidity does not engender Worms, because of their Bitterness which kills them.

The Juniper and the Cedar have the same Vertue of hindering Corruption: the Juniper by its Gum, which is call'd *Sandarax*, and the Cedar by its Oil call'd *Cedrium*.

The Larch-Tree has likewise the same Vertue, but its particular property is, that it will not burn. There is a remarkable Story of this Wood, which is, That when *Julius Cæsar* besieg'd a Castle at the Foot of the *Alpes*, there was a Tower built of this Wood, which prov'd the Principal Defence of the Place. He thought to take it easily by making a great Fire at the Foot of the Tower, but for all this great Fire, the Tower did not suffer the least Damage.

The Olive-Tree is likewise very serviceable, if it be put in the Foundations, and Walls of Cities; for after it has been singed a little, and interlaced among the Stones, it lasts for ever, and is out of all danger of Corruption.

Lime is made of White Stones or Flinty Pebbles, the harder the Stones are which 'tis made of, the better it is for Building. That which is made of soft Spongy Stones, is proper for Plastring.

There are five sorts of Sand; *viz.* Sand that is dug out of the Ground, River Sand, Gravel, Sea-Sand, and Pozzolana, which is a Sand peculiar to some Parts of *Italy*.

The best Sand is that which being rubb'd between the Hands makes a little Noise, which that Sand does not, which is Earthy, because it is not rough. Another Mark of good Sand is, that when 'tis put upon any Thing that is White and shak'd off, it leaves no Mark behind.

The Sand which is dug out of the Earth has all these Qualities, and is esteem'd the best. *Vitruvius* makes four sorts of it; *viz.* White, Black, Red, and Bright like a Carbuncle.

If it happen that there be no good Place to dig Sand in, we may make use of Sea-Sand, or River-Sand, which is likewise better for Plastering than the Sand which is digged, which is excellent for Building, because it drys quickly. Gravel likewise is very good, provided the grosser Parts be taken away. Sea-Sand is worst of all, because 'tis long adrying; and for this Reason, where 'tis made use of in Building, they are forc'd to desist sometimes till it dry.

The Sand which is found near *Naples* call'd *Pozzolana* is so proper to make good Mortar, if it be mixed with Lime, that not only in the ordinary Fabricks, but even in the very bottom of the Sea it grows into a wonderful hard Body. In Old Times they made use of it for Moles or Ports of the Sea, for after having made with Piles and Boards a Partition, they fill'd up the whole Compass of the Partition with this Mortar, which dry'd of it self in the middle of the Water and became a solid Body.

ARTICLE II.

Of the Use of the Materials.

Of the Preparation of Stone. Of Wood. Of Bricks. Lime and Sand.

The first thing we should have a Care of before we begin to build, is, to have the Stones dug out of the Quarry before they be used, and to expose them in some open Place, to the end that those which are endamaged by the Air, during this Time, may be put in the Foundation, and those that prove Durable and Good may be kept for the Walls above Ground.

We must likewise have a great care of the Wood which we make use of; That it be cut in a seasonable Time, which is in Autumn and Winter; for then it is not full of that superfluous Humidity which weakened it in dilating its Fibers, but it is firm and well closed by the Cold. This is so true, that the Wood of Trees which grow and become very great in a little Time, by reason of their great Humidity, is tender and apt to break, and very unfit for Building Which Experience shows us particularly in those Firrs call'd *Supernates*, which grow in *Italy*, on that side the *Apennine*, towards the *Adriatick*-Sea, for they are great and beautiful, but their Wood is not good for Building; whereas those on the other side of the Mountain, which are exposed to Heat and Dryness, call'd *Infernates*, are very good for Building.

This superfluous Humidity endamages Trees so much, that we are sometimes constrain'd to make a hole at the foot of the Tree and let it run out, which is the occasion of the Practice which is observ'd in cutting of Wood for Building, to Tap that Tree at the Foot, cutting not only the Bark, but even some part of the Wood it self, and so leave it for some time before it be Fell'd.

Lib. 1. Chap. 5.

It is likewise easie to judge of what great Importance the draining of this superfluous Humidity is for strengthning the Timber, and hindring Corruption, from this, That those Piles which are interlaced among the Stones in the Walls and Fortifications of Towns endure for ever without Corrupting, when they have been burnt a little on the outside.

Lib. 1. Chap. 11.

Lib. 2. Chap. 8.

Bricks ought not to be made use of but in very thick Walls; for this reason they did not build with Brick in *Rome*, for to save Ground; they were not permitted to make the Walls of their Houses above a Foot and a Half thick, which Makes about 16 Inches and a half of our Foot.

They likewise never made the top of their Walls with Brick; for the Brick of the Ancients not being baked, this part of the Wall would have been easily endamaged; for this reason they built it with Tiles, a foot and a half high, comprizing the Cornish or Entablature which was made likewise of Tiles to cast off the Water and defend the rest of the Wall. They likewise chose for these Cornishes the best Tiles, *viz.* those that had been long on the top of the Houses, and given sufficient Proof that they were well baked and made of good Matter.

The Walling with Brick was so much esteem'd among the Ancients, that all their Fabricks, as well publick as private, and their most beautiful Palaces were built with them. But that which principally made this sort of Building be esteem'd, was its great Duration; for when expert Architects were called to make an Estimate of Buildings, they always deducted an 80th. part of what they judged the Building cost for every Year that the Wall had been standing, for they supposed that the Walls could not ordinarily endure more than Fourscore Years; but when they valued Buildings of Brick, they always valued them at what they cost at first, supposing them to be of an Eternal Duration.

To make the right use of Lime and Sand, and to make good Mortar of them, it is necessary that the Lime be first well Quench'd, and that it be kept a long time, to the end that if there be any Piece of it that is not well burnt in the Kiln, it may, being extinguished at leasure, soften as well as the rest. This is of Great Importance particularly in Plastering and Works of *Stuck*, which is a Composition of Marble finely beaten with Lime. For if any little Pieces remain that are not well baked, when they come to be made use of, they crack and break the Work.

Lib. 7. Chap. 3.

The way to know whether the Lime be well Quench'd, is thus: You may thrust a Chip of Wood into it or a Knife, and if the Chip of Wood meet with any Stones, or that the Knife comes out clean without any sticking to it, it signifies the Lime was not will burnt; for when 'tis well Quench'd, it is Fat and will stick to the Knife; but the quite contrary happens to Mortar, for it is neither well prepar'd, nor well mix'd, if it stick to the Trowel.

Lib. 2. Chap. 4.

For to make the right use of Sand, you must first consider what it is to be employ'd in; for if it be Mortar for Plastring, you must not make use of Sand that was lately dug out, for it drys the Mortar too fast, which cracks the Plastring; but quite contrary if it be to be employ'd in Masonry, it must not have been a long time expos'd to the Air, for the Sun and the Moon do so alter it, that the Rain dissolves it, and turns it almost all into Earth.

Lib. 2. Chap. 5.

The Proportion that Sand and Lime ought to have to make good Mortar, should be three parts of Sand that is dug, or two parts of River-Sand or Sea-Sand against one of Lime, and 'twill be yet much better, if you add to the Sand of the Sea and the River a third part of Tiles well beaten.

Lib. 7. Chap. 3.

One of the Principal Things that is to be observ'd in making Mortar, is, to mix it well. The Grecian Workmen were so careful of this, that they Tewed it a great while, putting Ten Men to every Vessel wherein they wrought it, which gave so great a hardness to the Mortar, that when any big pieces of Plaster fell off the Old Walls, they made Tables of it.

ARTICLE III.

Of the Foundation.

In Foundations, to take care that the Earth be solid. Of the Masonry.

Lib. 6. Chap. 11.

The Foundation is the most important part of the Fabrick; for the Faults committed in it cannot be so easily remedied as in other parts.

Lib. 1. Chap. 5.

To lay the Foundation well, you must dig till you come to solid Ground, and even into the solid as much as is necessary to support the Weight of the Walls; it must be larger below than above the Superficies of the Earth.

Lib. 3. Chap. 3.

When you have found firm Earth to make it more solid, you must beat it with a Rammer; but if you cannot arrive at solid Earth, but find it still soft and spungy, you must dig as far as you can, and drive in Piles of Alder, Olive, or Oak, a little singed, near together, and fill up the void Places between the Piles with Coal.

Lib. 1. Chap. 5.

In short, you must make all Masonry with the most solid Stone that can be found for this use.

To make the Binding of the Stones the stronger in the Foundation of great Fabricks, you must put Piles of Olive a little singed and placed very thick from one Parement or Course to another, which serves, as it were, for Keys and Braces; for this Wood so prepar'd, is not subject to Worms, and will endure for ever, either in the Earth or in the Water, without the least Damage.

Lib. 6. Chap. 11.

When you would make Cellars, the Foundations must be much larger; for the Wall that is to support the Earth requires a greater thickness to resist the strong Efforts that the Earth makes against it in Winter, at which time it swells and becomes more heavy by reason of the Water it has drunk up.

ARTICLE IV.

Of the Walls.

Six sorts of Masonry. Precautions to be used in binding the Walls, to strengthen them with Wood. That they be exact perpendicular to ease them of their own weight, by Timber or Arches over doors and windows, and by Butresses in the earth.

Lib. 4. Chap. 2.

The right ordering of Stones joined with Mortar, which is call'd Masonry, is sevenfold; there are three of them which are of hewed Stone; *viz.* that which is in Form of a *Net*, that which is in *Binding*, that which is call'd the *Greek Masonry*. There are likewise three sorts of Masonry of unhewed Stones; *viz.* that which is of an *equal Course*; and that which is of an unequal, and that which is fill'd up in the middle; the seventh is compounded of all the rest.

The *Net-Masonry* is that which is made of Stones perfectly squar'd in their Courses, and are laid so, that the Joints go obliquely, and the Diagonals are the one Perpendicular, and the other Level. This is the most pleasing Masonry to the Sight, but it is apt to crack. See the Figure A. Table I.

The Masonry call'd the *Bound-Masonry*, is that, as *Vitruvius* explains it, in which the Stones are plac'd one upon another like Tiles; that is to say, where the Joints of the Beds are Level, and the Mounters are Perpendicular; so that the Joint that mounts and separates two Stones falls directly upon the middle of the Stone which is below.

Some Authors call this sort of Masonry *Incertain*, but they are mistaken; for they read *Incerta* instead of *Inserta*; it is not so Beautiful as the Net-work, but it is more solid and durable. See the Figure BB. Table I.

The Masonry which *Vitruvius* says is particular to the *Greeks*, is that, where after we have laid two Stones, each of which make a Parement or *Course*, another is laid at the end, which makes two Parements or *Courses*, and all the Building through observe this Order. This may be call'd *Double-Binding*; for the Binding is not only of Stones of the same *Course* one with another, but likewise of one *Course* with another *Course*. See Figure CC. Table I.

The manner of Walling by unequal Courses call'd *Isodomum* by the Ancients, differs in nothing from the Masonry call'd *Bound-Masonry*, but only in this, that the Stones are not hewed. See Figure D. Table I.

The other manner by unequal Courses call'd *Pseudisodomum* is also made of unhewed Stone, and laid in *Bound-Work*, but they are not of the same thickness, and there is no equality observ'd, but only in the several Courses, the Courses themselves being unequal one to another. See Figure A. Table I.

The Masonry which is fill'd up in the middle, call'd by the Ancients *Emplecton*, is likewise made of unhewed Stone and by Courses, but the Stones are only set in order as to the *Parements* or *Courses*, but the middle is fill'd up with Stones thrown in carelesly among the Mortar. See Fig. FF, GG, H. Table I.

Among all these sorts of Masonry, that will always be best which is made of Stones of an indifferent size, rather lesser than greater; to the end that the Mortar penetrating them in more parts may bind them faster, and the strength of the Mortar does not so soon decay. For we see that the Mortar which is laid in the Joints or Seams of the greater Stones with time decays and turns to Dust, which never happens to the most Ancient Fabricks which have been built of little Stones. From thence we may conclude, that it is ill Husbandry to be sparing of Mortar.

For this reason *Vitruvius* proposes another sort of Masonry, which may be call'd the *Compound Masonry*, for it is all the former together, of Stones hewed and unhewed, and fastned together with Cramp-Irons. The Structure is as follows: The *Courses* being made of hew'd Stone, the middle place which was left void is fill'd up with Mortar and Pebbles thrown in together; after this they bind the Stones of one *Parement* or *Course* to those of another with Cramp-Irons fasten'd with melted Lead. This is done to the end, that the abundance of Mortar which is in the middle may furnish and communicate a sufficient Humidity to the Joints of the great Stones which make the *Parements*. See the Figure K. Table I.

There are many Precautions to be given to make the Masonry more firm and durable, and these Precautions are common to all the different sorts of Masonry.

Lib. 1. Chap. 5.

When you would have the Walls very thick, for great and heavy Buildings, you must strengthen the inner part of the Wall with long Piles of singed Olive, which serves for Keys and Braces, for this Wood being so prepar'd never corrupts.

Lib. 6. Chap. 11.

Vide Index.

It is likewise of great Importance for the strength of Walls, that all be directly Perpendicular, and that the *Chains*, the *Pillars* and *Pieds-droits* or *Piers* be so situated, that *solid* always answer'd to the *solid*; for if there be any part of the Wall or any Pillar that carrys false, it is impossible the Work should continue long.

There are also two ways of strengthning the Walls, which are either to ease them of their own weight, or of that of the Earth which they are to support.

The first way of easing is in those Places where there are void spaces, as above Doors or Windows. These easements may be made two different ways; the first is to put over the Lintel which supports the Wall, which is over the void space of the Gates and Windows, two Beams, which lying or resting below directly upon *Pieds-*

droits or *Piers* meet together above.

The other way is, to make directly over the void spaces Vaulted Arches with Stones cut corner-ways and tending to one Center. For the Walls be so strengthned by the means of these easements, that part of the Wall which is below will not sink at all being easied of the load of the part that is above, and if some defect should happen by tract of time, it may be mended without propping that which is above.

The second way of easing, is, for Walls that are made to support the Earth; for, besides the extraordinary thickness which they ought to have, they should have likewise Buttresses on that side next the Earth, so far distant one from another as is the breadth of the Wall; they ought likewise to have an *Emparement* or large Foundation which must be equal to the height of the Wall, so that they go diminishing by degrees from the bottom to the top, where they come to equal the height of the Wall.

Lib. 1. Chap. 5.

The effect of these *Buttresses* is not only to support the Earth by their Resistance, but likewise to lessen its Efforts when it swells, in dividing it into many parts.

Lib. 6. Chap. 11.

And it be judg'd that these *Buttresses* be not sufficient, the Wall also which supports the Earth must be strengthned with other *Buttresses* within.

ARTICLE V.

Of Flooring and Ceiling.

Of Flooring upon the Ground between Stories. Open to the Air as Terrass, &c. the Roof. Cornice.

There are four sorts of Flooring, some are upon the *Superficies* of the Ground, others between two Stories, others make the Roof of the House in Platform, and the last is *Plat-Fond.*

To make those Floors that are upon the Ground, you must first make the Earth smooth and plain, if it be firm and solid, if not, it must be beaten with a Rammer with which they ram down their Piles; and after having cover'd the Earth with the first *Lay* or *Bed*, call'd *Statumen* by the Ancients, which was of Flinty Stones about the bigness of ones Fist, among which was mixed Mortar made of Lime and Sand. Then they laid the second *Bed*, which they call'd *Rudus*, which was made of lesser Stones, of which there were three Parts for one of Stone if they were new, for if they were taken out of old Buildings, five parts of Stones or Pibbles would be required for two of Lime.

Lib. 7. Cap. 4.

The *Greeks* had a way of making their Floors in those low places where cold and humidity ordinarily reign, which freed them from these Inconveniences. They digged the Earth two Foot deep, and after having beaten it well, they laid a Bed of Mortar or Cement a little sloping from either side to the Channel, which convey'd the Water under Ground; they laid a Bed of Coal upon the first Mortar, and having beaten them well, they cover'd them with another Cement or Mortar made of Lime, Sand and Ashes, which they made smooth when it was dry with a Polishing-Stone. These Floors presently drank up the Water that fell upon them, that one might walk barefoot without being incommoded by the Cold.

For the Floors which are between two Stories, there must be a particular care taken, that if there be any Partition below it, that it may not touch the Flooring for fear lest if the Flooring came to sink a little, it might be broke upon the Partition which remains firm.

Lib. 7. Cap. 4.

To make these Floorings, the Boards must be nailed at each end upon every Joist, to the end they may not warp; these Boards or Planks being cover'd with Straw, to hinder the Lime from wasting the Timber, the first Bed must be laid, made of a mixture of Mortar and little Stones a hand breadth, which must be beaten a long time with Iron-Levers, and so it must make a solid Crust which must be nine Inches thick; upon it shall be laid the *Noyau* or *Ame*, which must be at least six inches thick: It must be made of Cement, with which must be mix'd one part Lime for two parts of Cement. Upon the *Ame* or *Noyau* is placed the *Parement* made with the Rule, afterwards it must be scrap'd and all the Eminences and Inequality taken away: After that must be laid a Composition of Lime, Sand and beaten Marble, to fill equally all the Seams or Joints.

If a Flooring be to be made in the open Air, as upon *Terrasses*, that may endure Rain or Frost without any Damage; you must nail upon the Joists two Ranks of Boards across, one above the other; and having laid the first Bed, as is said before, it must be Paved with great Square Bricks two Foot Square, which must be hollow'd in the Ends in the Form of a half-Channel, the breadth of an Inch, which must be fill'd with Lime mixed with Oil. These Square Bricks must be higher in the middle, sloping two Inches for every six Foot; that is to say, a Forty-eighth Part. Upon these Square Bricks must be laid the *Ame*; upon which, after it has been well beaten, as well as the rest, must be put great Square Stones; and to hinder the Moisture from hurting the Boards, it is good to pour as much of the Lees of Oil as they will soak up.

Lib. 5. Chap. 10.

The under part of the Flooring, and the *Plat-Fonds*, must be made also with great Care. To make the *Plat-Fonds* or *Flat-roofs*, in the Form of a Vault, you must nail to the Joists of the Boards, or to the Rafters of the Roof, from two Foot to two Foot pieces of crooked Timber, and Choice must be made of Timber that is not apt to rot; such as, *viz. Cypress, Box, Juniper,* and *Olive*; no *Oke* must be made use of, because it will warp and crack the Work. The Joists being fastened to the *Suntmers*, you must fix to them *Spanish-Broom* with *Greek-Reeds* well beaten. These Reeds are in stead of Laths, which at present are made use of to make the Eaves of Houses;

over these Reeds must be laid a Plaster of Mortar, made of Sand, to hinder the Drops of Water which may fall from above from endamaging these *Plat-Fonds*. After which, the under part must be Plaster'd pretty thick, making all Places equal with Mortar made of Lime and Sand, that it may be afterwards Polished with Mortar made with Lime and Marble.

Lib. 5. Chap. 10.

The Ancients sometimes made double Vaults, when they were afraid that the Humidity which is engender'd, might rot the Wood which is upon by the Vapours which mount up the Vaults. This Method they principally made use of in their Baths.

The *Corniches* which are made use of under the *Plat-Fonds*, ought to be little, lest their great Jetting out, or Projecture should make them heavy, and apt to fall. For this Reason they ought to be made of pure Stuck of Marble, without any Plaster, that all the Work drying at the same time, may be less apt to break.

ARTICLE VI.

Of Plastering.

For great Walls, For Fresco. for Partitions. For moist places.

To make Plaster that it may continue a long time, and not crack; you must take Care to lay it on Walls that are very Dry; for if the Walls be Moist, the Plastering being expos'd to the Air, and drying faster than the Walls, will crack.

To do this Methodically, it must be laid, Bed after Bed, or Lay after Lay, having a great Care not to lay one Bed till the other be almost dry. The Ancients put six Lays, three of Mortar made of Lime and Sand, and three of Stuck. The first Lays or Beds were always thicker than the last, and they were very careful to make use of no Mortar made either of Sand or Stuck in their Plastring, that had not been a long time beaten and mix'd together; especially the Stuck, which must be beaten and mix'd till it will not stick to the Trowel.

They took likewise a great deal of Pains to run several times over and beat the Plaster, which gave it a Hardness, a Whiteness, and Polish'd it so well, that it shin'd like a Mirror.

These Plasterings so made, serve to Paint in *Fresco* upon; for the Colours being laid upon the Mortar before it was dry, pierced it, and Embodied with it; so that the Painting could not be defaced though it were wash'd; which would easily be wash'd off if the Mortar were dry.

They likewise laid these Plasterings upon Partitions of Wood filled with fat Earth, nailing Reeds to them, as we do Laths, and daubing it over with Clay, and then putting on another row of Reeds across upon the former, and another Bed of fat Earth or Clay, upon which they laid Beds of Mortar and Stuck, as we have said before.

Lib. 7. Chap. 4.

For the Plastering of low and moist places, they had a great many other Precautions, especially within the House; for as what belonged to the Out-part of the House, they contented themselves to Plaster from the Bottom of the Wall to the height of three Feet, with Cement.

But as to the Inward-parts of the House, when the Ground without was higher than the lowermost Flooring; they run up a little narrow Wall against the great one, leaving betwixt the two Walls only the distance of a Channel or Sewer, which they made lower than the Flooring, to receive the Water which might be gather'd against the Walls, and let it run out; and to the End they might hinder the gathering of much Water, by the Vapours which might be enclosed between these two Walls, they made towards the top of the little Wall Vents to let it out, and this little Wall was Plastered on the Out-side with Mortar and Stuck, as we have said before.

When the Place was too narrow to permit those Counter-Walls to be made within, they put hollow Tiles one upon another against the Wall, and placed and plaster'd them over with Mortar and Stuck. These Tiles which were Pitch'd over within, and were Demi-Channels, let the Water fall down into the Sewer, which sweat from the great Wall, and so let all the Vapours, which were engendred by Humidity, go out at the Vents.

CHAP. III.

OF THE CONVENIENCE OF FABRICKS.

ARTICLE I.

Of convenient Scituation.

That a place be convenient, it ought to be fertile, accessible, in a wholsom Air,
not on low Ground or marshy. How to know a wholsom Climate.

Lib. 2. Præs.

One of the Principal Things the Architect ought to consider, is the Convenience of the place where he would Build the Fabrick. This is the reason that *Dinocrates* was blamed by *Alexander*, for having propos'd him an Excellent Design for Building a City in a Barren place, and incapable of Nourishing those who were to Inhabit it.

We must then choose a place that is fertile, and hath abundance of every thing; and which hath likewise Rivers and Ports capable of furnishing it with all the Product and Commodities of the adjacent Countries.

The Third thing to be considered is, whether the Air be wholesome; and for this End, we must choose a high situated place, that it may be less Subject to Fogs and Mists; it must be likewise far from all Morasses, because the Corruption that may be caused by the infectious Breath of Venomous Beasts which commonly are ingendred there, makes the place very unwholsom, unless these Morasses be near the Sea, and situated high, that the Water may fall easily from them into the Sea, and that the Sea may likewise sometimes overflow them, and by its Saltness kill all the Venomous Beasts.

It is likewise to be remark'd, That a City situated upon the Sea, must needs have an unwholsom Air, if it be towards the South or the West; for generally the Heat weakens Bodies, and the Cold strengthens them; and so we see by Experience, that those who go out of a Cold Country into an Hot, have great difficulty to keep themselves in Health; whereas on the contrary, the Inhabitants of Hot Countries who go into Colder, have generally good Health.

The Ancients were accustomed to judge of the Quality of the Air, Water and Fruits, which might render a place wholsome by the Constitution of the Bodies of those Beasts which were nourished there, and to this End they consulted their

Entrails; for if the Liver was Corrupted, they conjectured that the same thing must happen to Men that should Inhabit in that place.

ARTICLE II.

Of the Form and Situation of the Building.

The Streets and Houses of a City to be the most advantagiously expos'd in respect to the Heavens and Wind. The scituation of each Room to be according to the use of it; of Dining-rooms, Libraries, Closets, &c.

Lib. 1. Chap. 6.

After having chosen a wholsome place, the Streets must be laid out according to the most Advantageous Aspect of the Heavens, and the best way will be to lay the Streets out so, that the Wind may not come directly into them, especially where the Winds are great and cold.

The Prospect of Private Mens Houses is made more or less Commodious, by the Openings which are differently made, to receive the Air and the Light according to the Quality of the Parts that are in the Fabrick.

Lib. 6. Chap. 9.

For the Cellars, Granaries, and generally all places that we wou'd Lock up, or keep any thing in, should be exposed to the North, and receive very few Rays of the Sun.

Lib. 6. Chap. 7.

The different Use of the Parts which Compose the Buildings, do likewise require different Situations; for the Dining-Rooms in Winter, and the Baths among the Ancients, were always turned to the West, for that Situation made them warmer, because the Sun then shone upon them, about the time they were wont to make use of those Apartments.

The Libraries ought to be turned to the rising Sun, because they are generally made use of in the Morning; besides, the Books are not so much damnified in Libraries so situated, as in those which are turned to the South and West, which are subject to Worms and a certain Humidity which engenders Moldiness, and consequently destroys the Books.

The Dining-Rooms for the Spring and Autumn, should be turned towards the East, to the end, that being covered from the great force the Sun hath when it is near Setting, they may be cooler about the time they are to be made use of.

The Summer Apartments must be turned to the North, that they may be fresher and cooler.

This Situation is likewise very proper for Closets, which are adorn'd with Pictures for the Light which is always equal, represents the Colours always alike.

There must likewise great respect be had to the difference of Climates, for the Excess of Heat and Cold, require different Situations and Structures; for the Houses in the Northern parts of the World, ought to be Vaulted, and have few Openings, and turn'd to the South; On the contrary in Hot Countries there must be great Openings and turn to the North; to the End that Art and Industry may remedy the Defects of the place.

ARTICLE III.

Of the Disposition of Fabricks.

The Dispositions of Buildings to be according to the use of the House, either publick or private; of Merchants Houses; of Country Houses; Of the several Apartments. Of Lights.

Lib. 6. Chap. 6.

The Disposition or Distribution of Fabricks contributes much to their Convenience, when each thing is so plac'd, that it is in a Proper place for the Use for which the Fabrick is Design'd; and for this reason the Town-House and the Market-Place ought to be in the Middle of the City, unless it happen that there be a Port or a River; for the Market ought not to be far distant from those places where the Merchandize is.

The Houses of Private Men, ought to be differently disposed, according to the divers Conditions of those that Dwell in them: For in the Houses of Great Men, the Apartments of the Lord, must not be at the Entry, where ought to be nothing but *Portico's, Courts, Peristyles, Halls,* and *Gardens* to receive the great Number of those who have Business with them, and make their Court to them.

The Houses of Merchants ought to have at the Entry their *Shops* and *Magazines,* and all other places where Strangers are to come about their Business.

Lib. 6. Chap. 9.

The Country Houses ought to have a different Order and Disposition from those of the City.

For the Kitchen ought to be near the Ox-house, so that from their Cratches they may see the Chimney and the rising Sun; for this makes the Oxen more Beautiful, and makes their Hair lie better.

The Baths ought likewise to be near the Kitchen, that the Water may be more conveniently heated.

The Press ought not to be far from the Kitchen, for that will much facilitate the Service that is necessary for the Preparation of Olives. If the Press be made of Wooden Beams, it ought to have at least for 16 Foot Breadth, 40 Foot of Length, if there be but one; or 24, if there be 2.

Not far from the Press, must the Cellar be plac'd, whose Windows must be turned to the North, because the heat spoils the Wine.

On the contrary, the Place where the Oil is kept, ought to be turned to the

South; to the End, the gentle heat of the Sun may keep the Oil from freezing.

The Houses for Sheep and Goats ought to be so large, that each of them may at least have 4 Foot for his place.

The Stables must likewise be Built near the House in a warm place, but not turned towards the Chimney; for Horses that often see the Fire, are generally ill Coated.

The Barns and Granaries, as likewise the Mills, ought to be at a pretty distance from the House, because of the Danger of Fire.

In all sorts of Fabricks, a particular Care must be taken that they be well lighted; but the Light is principally necessary in the *Stair-Cases*, *Passages*, and *Dining-Rooms*.

ARTICLE IV.

Of the Convenient Form of Buildings.

Of the Walls of Cities; Form of publick places which were different among the Greeks and Romans; of Stairs and Halls.

When we are assur'd of the Convenience of the place where the City is to be Built, by the Knowledge we have of the goodness of the Air, of its Fertility, Rivers and Ports, care must be taken to make Fortifications, which do not only consist in the Solidity of the Walls and Ramparts, but principally in their Form.

The Figure or Form of a place ought neither to be Square, nor Composed of Angles too far advanc'd, but it must have a great number of Corners, to the end the Enemy may be seen from all Parts; for the Angles that are so far advanc'd, are ill to be defended, and more favourable to the Besiegers than the Besieged. The Approach to the Walls must be made as difficult as possible.

The most Convenient Form of Publick Places, is to have in their Breadth 2 Thirds of their Length; The *Greeks* made about their Publick places *Double Portico's*, with Pillars near together, which Supported the Galleries above.

But the *Romans* finding this great number of Pillars to be inconvenient, placed them at a greater distance one from another, that they might have Shops well lighted.

Lib. 5. Chap. 3.

The Stair-Cases of all Publick Buildings, ought to be large and streight, and to have many Entrances, to the End the People may come in and out conveniently; but we shall speak of this more largely in another place.

Lib. 5. Chap. 2.

Lib. 6. Chap. 6.

The Halls where great Assemblies are to meet, ought to have their *Ceiling* very high, and to give them their true Proportion, we must unite the Length and Breadth, and give the half of the whole for the height of the *Ceiling*. The Halls where the *Ceiling* is not so high, must have only their breadth, and half of their length for their height.

Lib. 5. Chap. 2.

In vast and high places, to remedy the Inconvenience of the noisy Echo, about the middle of the height of the Wall, must be made a *Cornish* round about to break the course of the Voice; which without that, beating against the Walls, would beat a Second time against the *Ceiling*, and cause a troublesom double Echo.

CHAP. IV.

OF THE BEAUTY OF BUILDINGS.

ARTICLE I.

In what the Beauty of Building Consists.

Two sorts of beauty in Buildings; 1st, Positive, which consists in the Symme-
try, Materials, and Performance, 2d. Arbitrary, which is of two sorts; 1.
Prudence, 2. Regularity; which consist in the proper providing against
Inconveniences, and observing the Laws of Proportion. The beauty is
most seen in the proportion of these principal parts, viz. Pillars, Pied-
ments, and Chambrantes. From these things result two other, Gender
and Order.

*B*uildings may have two sorts of Beauty, the one *Positive,* and the other *Ar-*
bitrary. Positive Beauty, is that which necessarily pleaseth of her self; *Arbi-*
trary, is that which doth not necessarily please of her self, but her agreeableness
depends upon the Circumstances that accompany her.

Positive Beauty, consists in Three principal Things; *viz.* In the Equality of the Re-
lation that the Parts have one to another, which is called *Symmetry,* in the Richness
of the Materials, in the Properness, Neatness, and Exactness of the Performance.

Lib. 2. Chap. 8.

Lib. 1. Chap. 2.

Lib. 6. Chap. 11.

As to what regards the Relation of the Parts of the Fabrick one to another, *Vit-*
ruvius hath not spoke of it, but only where he prefers the *Netway* of Walling before
all other sorts of *Masonry,* because of the Uniformity that is in that Figure, and the
laying of the Stones; As to the Richness of the Materials, he leaves the Disposition
to him that is at the Expences of the Building; and he acknowledges that the Beau-
ty of the Performance depends wholly upon the Dexterousness and Industry of
the Workmen.

The second sort of *Beauty,* which only pleases by the Circumstances that ac-
company it, is of two sorts; The one is called *Wisdom,* and the other *Regularity.*
Wisdom consists in the reasonable use of *Positive Beauties,* which result from the
use and convenient ranking of the Parts; for the Perfection of which, to a rich and

precious Material, is given an Equal and Uniform Figure, with all the Property and Correctness possible.

Vitruvius gives us two Examples of this sort of *Beauty*; The first is, When *Bosses* or *Relievo's* are made to hide the Joynts, putting them directly under the *Bosses* which hide them by their jetting or projecture, for this gives them great Beauty and an agreeable Aspect.

The second is, When we consider the Winter-Appartments, that we have a care, that upon the Ceiling there be little or no Carving, and that the Ornaments be not made of Stuck, because it hath a shining whiteness, which will not endure the least nastiness; for it is impossible to hinder the smoak of the Fire and Candles which are lighted in the Winter, from tarnishing the beautiful Colour of the Work to which the Filth will stick, and enter into the Crevises of the Carving, which cannot be wiped out.

The *Regularity* depends upon the Observation of the Laws which are Established for the Proportions of all the Parts of *Architecture*, the Observation of these Laws extreamly pleases those that understand *Architecture*, who love these Proportions for two Reasons.

The First is, That they are for the most part founded upon Reason; which requires, for example, that the parts that support and are under, be stronger than those above; as we see in *Pedestalls*, which are broader than the Pillars they support, and they are broader at the bottom than the top.

The other Motive is *Prevention*, which is one of the most usual Foundations of the *Beauty* of all things, for even as we love the Fashion of the Cloaths which the Courtiers wear, although this mode have no *Positive Beauty*, but only for the Positive Merit of the Persons that wear them; so we are accustomed to love the Proportions of the Members of *Architecture*, rather because of the great Opinion that we have of them that Invented them, than for any *Positive Beauty* which is found in the Works of the Ancients, where these Proportions are observ'd; for often these Proportions are against Reason; as we may see in the *Thorus* of the *Ionick Base*, in the *Faces* of *Architraves* and *Chambranles*, or *Door-Cases*, with their *Mouldings*, where the Strong is supported by the Weak, and many other things, which Custom only hath made supportable.

These Proportions appertain to Three principal Members, which are *Pillars, Piedements, Chambranles*; the *Pillars* taken Generically, and as opposite to *Piedements*, and *Chambranles* or *Door-Cases*, have Three parts, *viz.* The *Pedestal*, the *Pillar*, and the *Ornaments*. Every one of these Parts is likewise divided into Three other Parts, for the *Pedestal* is composed of the *Basis*, its *Die* and its *Cornish*; the *Pillar* Comprehends its *Base, Shaft* and *Capital*. The *Ornaments* consist in the *Architrave, Frise*, and *Corniche*.

The *Piedement* or *Fronton*, has likewise Three Parts, *viz.* The *Tympan*, the *Corniches*, and the *Acroteres*. The *Chambranle* or *Door-Case* is composed of two *Piedsdroits*, or *Piers*, and the *Lintel* which also supports a *Frise*, which has likewise its *Cornich*.

The Disposition, Form, and different Proportions of all the Parts make two things, to which all that is Beautiful in Building hath a Relation, which is *Gender* and *Order*.

Gender depends of the Proportion, which is between the thickness of the *Pillars* and the space betwixt them.

Order, doth likewise depend in part upon the Proportion which is between the thickness of the *Pillars*, and their height; but we must likewise joyn to this Proportion many other things that appertain to the principal Parts of the *Pillars*, and other Parts which accompany it, such as are the *Gates*, the *Chambranles*, or *Door-Cases*; and other things which are different in different *Orders*.

ARTICLE II.

Of the Five sorts of Fabricks.

The five sorts are Pycnostyle, Systile. Diastyle, Areostyle, Eustyle. The Genders to be always agreable to the Orders of Architecture.

There are Five sorts of Fabricks; The First is called *Pycnostyle*, viz. where the Pillars are very close one to another, in such a Proportion that there is but from one Pillar to another, the space of a Diameter and half of the Pillar. See the *Fig.* AA. *Tab.* 2.

The Second is called *Systile*, viz. where the Pillars seem to be joyned together, are notwithstanding a little more distant one from another than in the *Pycnostile*; for the intercolumniation is two Diameters of the Pillars.

Lib. 2. Chap. 3.

The Defect that is observ'd in the *Systile* as well as in the *Pycnostile* is, that the Entrance of the Fabricks which are placed in that distance are very narrow: So that *Vitruvius* remarks that the Ladies as they walk to the Temple hand in hand, were forced when they came thither to quit one another, because they could not go two a Breast between the Pillars. See the Figure BB. Tab. II.

The Third is called *Diastyle*; *viz.* where the Pillars are further distant, the space of the Intercolumniation being three Diameters, and the Inconvenience is, that the space is so great, that the *Architraves* which lie upon the two Pillars are in danger of breaking; because the Ancients made them of one Stone. See Figure CC. Tab. II.

Lib. 3. Chap. 8.

The Fourth is called *Areostyle*; *viz.* where the Pillars are set very thin, there is no certain Proportion, but the distance of one Pillar from another, is much greater than that of *Diastyle*; and for this reason it can have no *Architrave* but of Wood. See the Figure DD. Tab. II.

The Fifth is called *Eustyle*; *viz.* where the Pillars are distant from one another by a more convenient Proportion than in any of the other kind. The distance consists of two Diameters of the Pillars, and one Fourth part of the Diameter: It has also this in particular, That the Intercolumniation in the middle is larger than the rest, having three Diameters of the Pillars; for this reason it surpasseth all others in Beauty, Solidity, and Convenience. See Tab. III.

Although the Essentials of these five Kinds, consist in the Proportion that is between the Diameter of the Pillar, and its Intercolumniation, they are also different by the Proportion which is between the Diameter of the Pillar and its height for the *Genders* or sorts, in which the Pillars are close one to another, ought to have the lesser Pillars; and in that kind, where the Pillars are in a greater distance one from another, they ought to be greater.

Lib. 4. Cap. 7.

But it's true, notwithstanding that these Proportions are not always observ'd, and that very often, to the *Ionick* and *Corinthian* Pillars, which are the smallest of all, Intercolumniations are given, which are proper to those of the *Thuscan Order*, where the Pillars are the greatest.

Lib. 3. Chap. 2.

But the Ordinary Practice is, to give to the Pillars of the *Areostyle* kind, the Magnitude of the 8th part of their height.

As to the *Diastyle* and *Eustyle*, the height is divided into Eight parts and an half, to give one to the breadth.

In the *Systyle* Kind, the Height is divided into Nine parts and an half, and one is given to the thickness.

In the *Picnostyle*, the thickness of the Pillar is the 10th part of the height, the reason of these different Proportions is founded upon this, that these Pillars do seem to lose of their thickness according as they are in Proportion great or long; and it's likewise for this Reason, that it is thought convenient to have the Pillars in the Corners thicker by a 50th part. See Tab. II. and Tab. III.

ARTICLE III.

Of the Five Orders of Architecture.

The distinction and difference in the several Orders; consists in the Strength and Ornament; Vitruvius speaks but of three Orders.

The Five Orders of Architecture are, the *Thuscan*, the *Dorick*, the *Ionick*, the *Corinthian*, and the *Compound*.

These Orders were Invented to satisfie the Design that might be had of making Fabricks more or less Massy, and more or less adorn'd, for the Distinction of these Orders consists in two things, that as the *Thuscan* and *Dorick* Order are more massy and less adorn'd, so the *Corinthian* and *Compound* are Slenderer and Richer, the *Ionick* holds the Middle, as well in its Proportions, as its Ornaments, being less massy and more adorn'd than the *Thuscan* and the *Dorick*, and more massy and less adorn'd than the *Compound* and the *Corinthian*.

Lib. 4. Chap. 1. Præf. 4.

Lib. 4. Chap. 7.

Though *Vitruvius* hath only divided Architecture into Three Orders; *viz.* The *Dorick*, the *Ionick* and the *Corinthian*; he doth not for all that forget to give the Proportions of the *Thuscan*, and speak of the *Compound*.

ARTICLE IV.

Of Things that are Common to several Orders.

There are seven things common to all Orders, viz. Steps. Pedastals, the diminution of Pillars, the Channelings of Pillars, which is of three sorts, the Piedemont. Cornices, and Acroteres.

Before we treat of the Differences of these Five Orders, it would be proper to speak of those Things that are common to several Orders; as are the *Steps, Pedestals,* the *Diminution of Pillars,* their *Channelling, Piedements, Cornices,* and *Acroteres.*

Lib. 3. Chap. 3.

The *Steps* which are before the Temple, ought always to be of an the end, that having put the right Foot in mounting the first *Step*, it may likewise be upon the last.

They ought not to be more than 6 Inches 10 Lines high, nor less than 6 Inches.

Lib. 9. Chap. 2.

Their breadth ought to be proportion'd to their height, and this Proportion ought to be of 3 to 4; so that if the *Steps* be 6 parts high, which is 3 times 2, they must be 8 broad, which is 4 times 2; following the Proportion of a Triangular Rectangle invented by *Pythagoras.*

Lib. 3. Chap. 3.

The Landing-places ought not to be narrower than 16 Inches and an half, nor broader than 22 Inches, and all the *Steps* that are round about a Fabrick should be all of the same breadth.

The *Pedestals* which support many Pillars of the same Rank, will be much handsomer if one make them jet out before every Pillar like a Joynt-Stool; for otherwise, if the *Bases* were all of one size, they would resemble a Channel.

If Leaning-places, or Elbow-places are to be betwixt the *Pedestals*, it's necessary that they be as high as the *Pedestals*, and that the *Cornices* of the *Pedestals*, and of the Leaning or Elbow-places be equal, and have a true Proportion one to another.

Lib. 5. Chap.1.

Lib. 3. Chap. 2.

All the Pillars ought to go diminishing towards the top, to augment their Strength, and render them more Beautiful, imitating the Bodies of Trees, which are greater at the Bottom than at the Top. But this *Diminution* must be lesser in the great Pillars which have their highest part further from the Sight, and which by Consequence makes them at the top seem lesser, according to the ordinary Effect of Perspective; which always diminisheth Objects according to the measure that they are distant from the Eye.

The Rule of this different *Diminution* is, that a Pillar that is 15 Foot high, ought to have in the upper part 5 parts of 6 in the which the Diameter of the *Base* of the Pillar is divided; that which is from 15 to 20 Foot, ought to have 5 and an half of the 6 and an half of the Diameter; that which is from 20 to 30, ought to have 6 of the 7 parts of the Diameter; that which is from 30 to 40, must have 6 and an half of 7 and an half of the Diameter; that which is from 40 to 50, must have 7 of 8 of the Diameter. These *Diminutions* do not belong to the *Thuscan Order*, whose Pillars are much more diminished; as we shall show hereafter.

Lib. 3. Chap. 3.

Besides this *Diminution* which is made towards the top of the Pillar, there is another below, which makes the Pillar about the middle swell like a Belly; the measure of this swelling is taken from the magnitude which makes up the Distance between the *Channels*.

Lib. 3. Chap. 2.

There is another sort of *Diminution of Pillars*, which ismade of one Pillar in respect of another; It is of 2 sorts, *viz.* when a second rank is placed upon the first, for then the second Pillar must be lesser a fourth part than those below, or when *Portico's* are made that have Pillars in the Corners, for those in the middle must be less than those in the Corners, a 50th part.

Lib. 4. Chap. 1.

The *Channellings* are so called, because they are as itwere *Demi-Channels*, which descend from the top of the Pillar to the bottom; they represented the Plaites of the Garments of Women, which the Pillars resembled.

Lib. 4. Chap. 3.

There are three sorts of *Channellings*, the two first are particular and proper to the *Dorick Order*; the third is common to the *Ionick, Corinthian* and *Compound*: The two first are more plain and simple, and fewer in number than the others.

The most Simple is that which is not hollowed at all, and which hath only *Pans* and flat Fronts or Faces.

Lib. 3. Chap. 3.

The other is a little hollowed; to make this hollowness, a Square must be made, whose Side must be equal to the *Pan*, in which the *Channelling* is to be made, and having put one foot of the Compass in the middle of the Square, make a crooked Line from one Angle of the *Channelling* to the other, both these *Channellings* are made up to the number of Twenty.

Lib. 4. Chap. 1.

Lib. 4. Chap. 4.

The other Orders have 24, and sometimes 32, when it is design'd to make the Pillars seem greater than they are; for the Eye judgeth that all things are greater when they have more and different Marks, which lead as it were the Sight to more Objects at once.

These *Channellings* are deeper than those of the *Dorick Order*, and the depth ought to be just so much, that a Carpenter's Rule being put into the Cavity, touch with its Angle the bottom, and with its sides the two Corners of the *Channelling*. *Vitruvius* hath not taught us what the Proportions of the *Channelling* should be, in respect of the *Fillet* which makes up the space between the *Channellings*, nor what the breadth of the *Fillet* should be, which he hath establish'd for the rule of the swelling Belly of the Pillar.

The *Piedement* is composed of a *Tympan* and *Cornices*; to have the true height of the *Tympan*, we must divide the breadth which is between the two ends of the *Cymatium* of the *Larmier*, or *Drip* which supports the *Piedement*, into 9 parts, and give one to the *Tympan*.

The thickness of the *Cornice* being added to this 9th part, makes up the height of the whole *Piedement* or *Fronton*.

The *Tympan* ought to be Perpendicular upon the *Gorge* of the Pillar, the things that are common to all *Cornices* are, that the *Cornice* of the *Piedement* must be equal to that below, excepting the last great *Cymatium*, which ought not to be upon the *Cornice* below the *Piedement*, but it ought to go over the *Cornices* which are sloping upon the *Piedement* or *Fronton*.

This great *Cymatium* ought to have of height an 8th part more than the *Crown*, or *Drip*, or *Larmier*.

In places where there are no *Piedements*, in the great *Cymatiums* of the *Cornices*, must be cut the Heads of Lions, at such a distance, that there must be one directly upon every Pillar, and that the other answer directly upon the great *Dalles*, that cover the House. These Heads of Lions are pierced through to convey the Water which falls from the Roof upon the *Cornice*: The Heads of the Lions which are not directly upon the Pillars, ought not to be pierced, to the end the Water may flow with the greater impetuosity through those which are directly upon the Pillars, and that it may not fall between the Pillars upon those who are to go into the *Portico's*.

The *Greeks* in their great Buildings never put any *Dentels* under the *Modillons*, because the *Rafters* could not be under the *Forces*, or *Sheers*, and it is a great fault that That, which according to the true Rules of Building ought to be placed above, should be placed under in the Representation.

For this Reason, the Ancients never approved of *Modillons* in the *Piedements*, nor of *Dentels*, but only simple *Cornices*; for neither the *Forces*, *Sheers*, nor the *Rafters* can be represented in the *Piedements*, out of which they cannot jet but only directly out of the Eaves of the House upon which they lie sloping.

The *Acroteres* are three *Pedestals*, which are upon the Corners and Middle of the *Piedement* to support Statues; those of the Corner ought to be as high as the Middle of the *Tympan*; but the *Acrotere* in the middle ought to be higher by an 8th part than the other.

All the Members or Parts which shall be placed upon the Capitals of Pillars, *viz. Architraves*, *Frises*, *Cornices*, *Tympans*, and *Acroteres*, should encline forward the 12th part of their height.

There is likewise another General Rule; which is, that all the parts that jet out, should have their Projecture equal to their Height.

ARTICLE V.

Of the Thuscan Order.

The Tuscane Order consists in the Proportion of Columns, in which there are three parts, the Base, the Shaft, and the Capital. Of Chambrantes; and of the Piedement.

It hath been said that all Buildings have three Parts, which may be different according to the divers Order, *viz.* The *Pillars*, the *Piedements*, and the *Chambranles*, or *Door-Cases*; and that the *Pillars* had three Parts, which are the *Pedestal*, the *Shaft*, and its Ornaments, *viz.* The *Architrave*, the *Frise* and the *Cornice*.

Neither the Proportion of the *Pedestals*, nor of the *Gates* and *Chambranles* of the *Thuscan Order* are to be found in *Vitruvius*.

Lib. 4. Chap. 7.

The Proportion of the Pillar is this, that its thickness below is the 7th part of its height, it's Diminution is the 4th part of the Diameter of the Pillar, its *Base* has half of the Diameter of the Pillar for its height, the *Plinthus* being round, makes one half of the *Base*; the other half is for the *Thorus*, and for the *Conge* or *Apophygis*, Vid. *Conge* explained.

The height of the Capital is half the Diameter of the Pillar, the breadth of the *Abacus* is equal to the whole Diameter of the Pillar at the bottom, the height of the Capital is divided into three Parts; one of them is allowed the *Plinthus*, which serves instead of an *Abacus*; the *Echine* hath another; and a third Part is for the *Gorge* of the Capital comprehending the *Astragal*, the *Conge*, or *Apophygis*, which are immediately under the *Echine*.

Upon the Pillars must be laid the *Sabliers*, or *Wooden Architrave*, joyned together by *Tenons*, in the form of a Swallows Tail.

These *Sabliers* ought to be distant one from another about an Inch; for if they should touch one another, the Timber would heat and corrupt.

Upon these *Sabliers* which serve for an *Architrave*, must be built a little Wall, which will serve instead of a *Frise*.

The *Cornice* which is laid upon this little Wall or *Frise*, has *Mutal's* which jet out.

All the Crowning should have the 4th part of the height of the Pillar. The little Walls that are built between the ends of the Beams which rest upon the Pillars, must be garnished and covered with Boards, which must be nailed upon the ends of the Beams.

The *Piedement*, which may be either of Stone or Wood, and which must support the *Faistag* or *Top*, the *Forces*, and the *Pans*, has a particular Proportion; for it must be much raised to give it a sufficient sloping for the running of the Water. See Tab. V.

ARTICLE VI.

Of the Dorick Order.

The Dorick Order consists in the proportion; of the Columns, which have been different at diverse times, and in diverse Works. The parts of the Column are the Shaft; the Base which it anciently wanted, but hath since borrowed from the Attic; the proportion of the Base, and the Captial, the Archiatrave, which hath two parts, the Platbands and the Gouttes, the Frise, in which are the Triglyphs and the Metops, the Proportion of them. Of the Cornice, its proportion.

Lib. 4. Chap. 1.

The *Dorick* Pillar has had in divers times, and in different Buildings, different Proportions; for at first it had only for its height 6 times its Diameter; this Proportion imitating that of Humane Bodies, in which the length of the Foot is the 6th part of all the Body, afterwards they allowed 7 times its Diameter.

Lib. 5. Chap. 9.

But this Proportion that the Pillars of the Temples had at the Beginning, was afterwards changed in that of the Theaters, where they were higher by half a Diameter; for they made them 15 Modules high, for in the *Dorick Order* the Semi-Diameter of the Pillar at the bottom is the Module, which in other Orders is a whole Diameter.

Lib. 4. Chap. 1.

The *Dorick* Pillar is composed as well as the rest of a *Shaft*, *Base* and *Capital*, though *Vitruvius* makes no mention of the *Base*; and it's easie to conclude, that in the Ancient Buildings this *Order* had none; for it is said, That when they would make the *Ionick Order* more Beautiful than the *Dorick*, they added a *Base* to it; and there is yet to be seen in Ancient Buildings of this Order, Pillars without a *Base*; but when a *Base* is added to it, it must be *Attick Base*, whose Proportion is as follows.

The whole *Base* ought to have a *Module* for its height; that is to say, half the Diameter of the Pillar; this *Module* being divided into three parts; one is for the *Plinthus*; the other two parts are divided into four, of which one is allowed for the upper *Torus*, the three which remain, are divided into two: The half below is for the lower *Torus*, the other is for the *Scotiæ*, comprising the two little Squares or Filets. The breadth of the *Basis* in General is a 4th of the Diameter of the Pillar at the bottom, added on every side; but this jetting is excessive, and without any Example, and *Vitruvius* himself makes it lesser in the *Ionick Base*.

Lib. 4. Chap. 3.

The height of the *Capital* as well as the *Base* is one *Module*, the breadth is two *Modules* and an half, the height of the *Capital* being divided into three parts, one must be allowed for the *Plinthus* or *Abacus*, with its *Cymatium*; the other is for the *Echine*, with its *Anulets*; the third appertains to the *Gorge* of the *Capital*.

The Architrave which comprehends its *Platte-Band* with the *Gouttes* or *Pendant Drops*, which are under the *Triglyphs*, is as well as the *Capital* of one only *Module*; the *Gouttes* or *Drops* with their little *Tringle*, ought to have the 6th part of a *Module*, the breadth under the *Architrave* ought to be equal to that above the Pillar.

Upon the *Architrave* in the *Friese* ought to be the *Triglyphs* and the *Metops*. The *Triglyphs* have a *Module* and a half for their height, and a *Module* for their breadth; the *Metops* are as high as broad; One *Triglyph* must be placed directly upon every Pillar, and the Intercolumniation ought to have three; towards the Corners must be placed the *Demi-Metops*.

The breadth of the *Triglyph* being divided into six parts, five of them must be left in the middle, and the two halfs which remain on the right and the left, must be for *Demi-Graveurs*; The part in the middle, and the two last of the five, must be for the three Feet, and the two which are betwixt the three Feet, must be for the *Graveurs* or *Channels*, which must be hollowed, following the Corner of the Mason's Rule. The *Capital* of the *Triglyph* ought to have the 6th. part of a *Module*.

Upon the *Capital* of the *Triglyph* is placed the great *Cornice*, its Jetting or Projecture, is half a *Module* and the 6th. part of a *Module*, its height is half a *Module*, comprising the *Dorick Cymatium*, which is under it.

On the *Plat Fonds* of the *Cornice*, must be hollowed little strait ways, which must answer perpendicularly to the sides of the *Triglyphs*, and the middle of the *Metops*.

Streight upon the *Triglyphs* must be cut 9 *Goutes* or *Drops*, which must be so distributed, that there may be six length-wise, and three broad-wise; in the Spaces which are betwixt the *Metops*, because they are greater than those between the *Triglyphs*: nothing must be cut unless it be *Foudres*. Moreover towards the border of the Crown must be Carved a *Scotia*.

Some advance perpendicularly above the *Triglyphs*, the Ends of the *Forces* or *Principals* to frame the *Mutils* which support the *Cornices*; so that as the Disposition of *Beams* hath caused the Invention of *Triglyphs*, so the jetting of the *Forces* hath caused the Disposition of the *Mutils*, which support the *Cornices*. See Tab. VI.

ARTICLE VII.

Of the Ionick Order.

The preportion of Pillars of this Order. The Pillars set upon the Bases two ways, perpendicular, and not so. Proportion of the Base, divided into its parts the Plinthus, the Thorus, the Scotia upper and lower, with the Astragals. Of the Capital, its proportion and parts. Of the Architrave, wherein to be considered, the proportion it must have to the Pedestals, and to the heighth of the Column, to the breadth at the bottom, and to the jetting of the Cymatium. Of the Frise and Cornice.

Lib. 4. Chap. 1.

The Proportion of the Pillars of the *Ionick Order* in the beginning had Eight *Modules* or Diameters for their height, but the Ancients quickly added half a Diameter, when to make this Pillar more Beautiful than the *Dorick*, not only for its height, but also for its Ornaments, they added a *Base* to it, which was not used in the *Dorick Order*.

The Pillars must be set upon their *Bases* two ways; for sometimes they were perpendicularly set, and sometimes not, *viz.* The outward rows of Pillars; when there were more Ranks than one; for that part of the Pillar which is towards the Wall of the Fabrick must necessarily be perpendicular, and the outward part must have all the Diminution, and must lean towards the Wall.

Lib. 3. Chap. 3.

The Pillars that are within the porch, and are betwixt the Wall and the outward Pillar must stand perpendicularly.

The breadth of the *Ionick Base* is the Diameter of the Pillar, to which is added a 4th. and an 8th. part; its height is half the Diameter; its height being divided into three parts, one is allowed for the *Plinthus*, the rest being divided into seven parts, three are allowed to the *Torus* above, after equally dividing the four which remain, the two above are for the upper *Scotia*, with its *Astragal*: The two below are for the lower *Scotia*, which will appear greater than the upper, because it extends to the edge of the *Plinthus*, the *Astragals* must have the 8th. part of the *Scotia*, whose Jetting or Projecture must be the 8th. part of the whole *Base* joyned to the 6th. part of the Diameter of the Pillar. See Tab. VII.

As to the *Capital*, the *Abacus* must have in its Square the Diameter of the bottom of the Pillar, adding to it an 18th. part; half of the *Abacus* ought to be the height of the *Capital*, comprizing the Round of the *Volute* or *Scroll*, but there must be substracted from the corner of the *Abacus* a 12th. part and an half of the height of the *Capital*, and after the whole thickness of the *Capital* must be divided into nine parts and an half, and one and an half must be left for the thickness of the *Abacus*, that the *Volutes* or *Scrolls* may be made of the eight which remain; then having left under the *Abacus* four parts and an half of these eight, a Line must be drawn in the place which cuts the two a-cross and the Points of the Section shall be *Eyes*, which shall have eight parts for their Diameter; in half the space of the *Eye* shall be placed the Centers through which shall be drawn with a Compass the Spiral-Line of the *Volute*, beginning the height under the *Abacus*, and going into the four Quarters of the Division, diminishing till we come directly to the first Quarter, and giving to every Quarter a particular Center.

Then the thickness of the whole *Capital* must be so divided that of nine parts which it contains, the *Volute* has the breadth of three under the *Astragal*, on the top of the Pillar, which must be directly upon the *Eye* of the *Volute*, that which remains above the *Astragal*, must be allowed for the *Abacus, Channel*, and the *Echine* or *Egge*, whose jetting beyond the Square of the *Abacus* must be of the same bigness of the *Echine* or *Egge*.

The *Channel* must be hollowed the 12th. part of its breadth.

The *Girdle* or *Cincture*, or the lateral part of the *Capital*, ought to advance out of the *Tailhoir Abacus*, as much as it is from the Center of the *Eye* to the height of the *Echine*.

The thickness of the *Axis* of the *Volutes*, which is the thickness of the *Volute*, seen sideway, and which makes up the extreme parts of that which is called commonly *Balisters*, ought not to exceed the magnitude of the *Eye*. See Tab. VIII.

These Proportions of the *Ionick Capital*, are only for Pillars of 15 Foot, those that are greater require other, and generally the greater Proportions are required for the Pillars that are greater; and for this reason we have said, that the higher the Pillars are, the less Diminution they must have; so when the Pillars are above 15 Foot, we must add a 9th. part to the Diameter of the Pillar for to give the breadth to the *Abacus*; to which is never added more than an 18th. part to Pillars of 15 Foot.

The *Architraves* shall be laid upon the Pillars with Jettings equal to the *Pedestals*, in case they be not all of one size, but in form of Joint-Stools, to the end Symmetry may be observ'd.

The height ought to be different, according to the proportion of the height of the Pillar; for if the Pillar be from 12 to 15 Foot, we must allow the *Architrave* the height of half a Diameter of the bottom of the Pillar, if it be from 15 to 20, we must divide the height of the Pillar into 15 parts, to the end we may allow one to the *Architrave*; so if it be from 20 to 25, the height must be divided into 12 parts and an half, that the *Architrave* may have one; and so proportionably.

The *Architrave* ought to have at the bottom which lies upon the *Capital*, the same breadth that the top of the Pillar hath under the *Capital*.

The Jetting of the *Cymatium* of the *Architrave* ought to answer the bottom of the Pillar, the height of the *Cymatium* ought to be the 7th. part of the whole *Architrave*.

The rest being divided into 12 parts; three must be allowed to the first *Face*, four to the second, and five to that above, upon which is the *Cymatium*.

The *Frise* ought not to be so high as the *Architrave* by a 4th. part, unless something be carved there, for then that the Carving may be more graceful, the *Frise* ought to be bigger than the *Architrave* by a 4th. part.

Upon the *Frise* must be made a *Cymatium* of height the 7th. part of the *Frise*, with a Jetting equal to its height.

The *Dentil* which is upon the *Cymatium*, shall have the height of the *Face* of the middle of the *Architrave*, with a Jetting or Projecture equal to its height; the cutting of the *Dentils* ought to be so made, that the breadth of every *Dentil* may be the half of its height, and the Cavity of the cut which is between every *Dentil* may have two parts of three, which maketh the breadth of the *Dentil*.

The *Cymatium* which is upon the *Dentil*, must have the 3d. part of the height of the *Dentil*.

The Crown with its little *Cymatium* must have the same height with the *Face* of the middle of the *Architrave*.

The great *Cymatium* ought to have the height of an 8th. part more than the *Crown* or *Drip*.

The Jetting or Projecture of the whole *Cornice* comprehending the *Dentil* ought to be equal to the space that there is from the *Frise*, just to the top of the great *Cymatium*, and generally speaking all the Jettings or Projectures shall have the better grace when they are equal to the height of the Jetting Members. See Table VII.

ARTICLE VIII.

Of the Corinthian Order.

This Order different from the Ionick in nothing but in the Capitals of Pillars, being otherwise composed of the Dorick and Ionick; the proportion of the Capital, in which are to be consider'd its heighth, its breadth at the bottom, the Leafs, Stalks, the Volutes, and the Roses. Of the Ornaments.

Lib. 4. Chap. 2.

The Pillars of the *Corinthian Order* have no other Proportions than the *Ionick*, except in the *Capital*, whose height make them appear slenderer and higher. The other parts or Members, as the *Architrave*, *Frise*, and *Cornice*, borrow their Proportions from the *Dorick* and *Ionick Order*, having nothing particular, for the *Corinthian Modillons* are imitated by the *Mutils* of the *Dorick Order*, and the *Dentils* are the same with the *Ionick*; this being so, we have nothing to do but to give the Proportions of the *Capital*, which are these; The *Capital* comprizing the *Abacus*, hath for its height, the breadth of the bottom of the Pillar.

To have the true breadth of the *Abacus*, we must have a care that its *Diagonal* be double the height of the *Capital*, the bending that the sides of the *Abacus* have inward, is a 9th. part of a side, the bottom of the *Capital* is equal to the Neck of the Pillar. The thickness of the *Abacus* is a 7th. part of the whole *Capital*.

Two of these seven parts must be taken for the height of every Leaf, of which there are two Ranks, each of which has four Leaves.

The Stalks or little Branches are likewise composed of other Leaves, and which grow between the Leaves of the Rank above, ought to have two of these seven parts comprising the *Volutes*.

These *Volutes* begin within the Stalks, of which, those that are the greatest extend to the Extreme parts of the *Angles* of the *Abacus*; the other are below the *Roses*.

These *Roses* which are in the middle of every *Face* of the *Abacus*, ought to be as great as the *Abacus* is thick.

The *Ornaments* of the *Corinthian Order*, viz. The *Architrave*, the *Frise*, and the *Cornice*, do not in the least differ from those of the *Ionick Order*. See Tab. IX.

ARTICLE IX.

Of the Compound Order.

The Compound is not described by Vitruvius, it being a general Design, and borrows the parts of the Capital (which is the only distinction it has) from the Corinthian, Ionick, and Dorick Orders.

Lib. 4. Chap. 1.

*V*itruvius hath not spoke of the *Compound Order*, as of an *Order* distinct from the *Corinthian*, the *Ionick* and the *Dorick*; He only tells us, that sometimes upon the *Corinthian Pillar* was placed a *Capital* composed of several parts, which were taken from the *Corinthian*, the *Ionick* and *Dorick Orders*.

But a Consequence may be drawn from thence, that the *Order* at present called the *Compound*, might have been in use in the time of *Vitruvius*, although they then did not make a distinct *Order* of it; Since that, our *Compound Order* is not essentially different from the *Corinthian*, but by its *Capital*; and so one may say, that this sole difference of the *Capital* ought to make it a distinct *Order* from the *Corinthian*, since according to *Vitruvius*, the *Corinthian Capital* alone, made the *Corinthian Order*.

The parts that our *Compound Order* borrow from the *Corinthian Order*, are the *Abacus*, and the two Ranks of the Leaves of *Branch-Ursin*, which it has retained, although the *Corinthian* have quitted them for the Leaves of the *Olive*.

The other part that it takes from the *Ionick*, are the *Volutes*; which it forms in some manner according to the Model of the *Volutes* of the *Corinthian Order*, in bending them even as the *Abacus*; for they are direct upon the *Ionick Capital*, as well as the *Abacus*.

The *Echine*, or Quarter Round, which it has under the *Abacus*, it borrows rather from the *Dorick Order*, than from the *Ionick*; because this *Echine* is immediately under the *Abacus*, as it is in the *Dorick Order*, which is not in the *Ionick*, which between the *Echine* and the *Abacus*, places the *Channel* which makes the *Volute*; it may notwithstanding be said, that it imitates the *Echine* of the *Ionick Order*, in that it is cut with *Oves* or *Eggs*, which is rarely found in the *Dorick Capital*, but are always in the *Ionick*.

PART II.
CONTAINING THE ARCHITECTURE PECULIAR TO THE ANCIENTS.

CHAP. I.

OF PUBLICK BUILDINGS.

ARTICLE I.

Of Fortresses.

In Fortification four things are consider'd; the disposition of the Ramparts; the Figure of the whole place, the building of the Walls; thickness, materials, and terrass; the figure and disposition of the Towers.

Lib. 1. Cap. 3.

Buildings are either *Publick*, or *Private*; Those that are Publick, appertain either to Security, or Religion, or Publick Convenience. The Fortifications of Cities are for *Security*, the Temples for *Religion*, the Market-places, Town-Houses, Theatres, Academies are for the *Publick Convenience.*

The Disposition and Figures of the Ramparts were so ordered, that the Towers advanced out of the Walls to the end, that when the Enemy approached them, the Besieged which were in the Towers, might fall upon their Flank, both on the Right and the Left.

They took likewise great Care to make the Approaches to the Walls difficult, ordering their Ways so, that they came not directly, but to the Left of the Gate. For by this means, the Besiegers were constrained to present to them that were upon the Walls the Right side, which was not covered with a Buckler.

The Figure of a *strong* place ought neither to be Square, nor composed of Angles that advance too far. But the Ancients made them with many Sinuosities or Corners, for Angles that are too far advanc'd, are more advantageous for the Besiegers, than the Besieged.

The thickness of the Wall was so ordered, that two Armed Men might walk by one another upon the Wall without justling.

They made their Walls strong and durable, with sindged Beams of Olive, which bound them and kept them up.

Although there be nothing that makes the Ramparts so strong as Earth, they had not for all that the Custom of making Terrasses, unless it were in some place where some Eminency was so near the Wall, that the Besiegers might easily enter.

To make the Terrasses strong, and to hinder the Earth from pushing down the two Walls that supported it, they made Buttresses or Counter-forts which went from one Wall to another, to the end, that the Earth being divided into many parts, might not have that weight to push the Walls.

Their Towers were round, for those that are square are easily ruin'd by their War-like Engines, and their Battering easily broke down the Corners.

Directly against the Tower, the Wall was cut off within the breadth of the Tower, and the Walls so interrupted were only joyned with Joyces, which were not nailed down; to the end, that if the Enemy made themselves Masters of some part of the Wall, the Besieged might take up this Bridge made of Joists, and hinder their further advance.

ARTICLE II.

Of Temples.

Temples divided in the Greek and Tuscan Fashion; of the Greek some were round, and some square; in the square Temples of the Greeks three things are to be considered; 1. the Parts, which are five, the Porch, the Posticum, the Middle, the Portico, and the Gates, which were of three sorts, viz. Dorick, Jonick, and Attick. 2. The Proportion, and 3. The Aspect, in respect to the Heavens, and to its own parts, which were different in Temples with Pillars, and those without Pillars; of Temples with Pillars there are eight sorts. Round Temples were of two sorts, Monoptere, Periptere. Temples of the Tuscane Fashion. The Ancients had fourteen sorts of Temples.

Lib. 4. Chap. 4.

The second Sort of Publick Fabricks, which are those that belong to Religion are the *Temples*, which among the Ancients were of two Sorts; some were after the *Greek*, and some after the *Tuscan* Fashion.

The *Temples* after the *Tuscan* Fashion were Square, the *Greeks* made them sometimes Round, sometimes Square; in the Square *Temples* of the *Greeks*, there are three Things to be considered, *viz.* The Parts that compose it, the Proportion of the *Temple*, and its *Aspect*.

The Parts of the Square *Temples*, were for the most part Five; for they had almost every one of them a Porch before the Temple called *Pronaos*, and another Porch behind the *Temple*, called *Posticum*, or *Opisthedomos*, the middle of the *Temple*, called *Cella*, or *Sacos*; the *Portico's* or *Isles*, and the *Gate*.

The Porch was a place covered at the Entrance at the greatest part of *Temples*, being as broad as the whole *Temple*. There were three sorts of them. Some were surrounded with Pillars on three Sides; Others had only Pillars in the Front, the Sides of the Porch being made up by the continuation of the Side-Walls of the *Temple*; Others were made up at the Sides, partly by Pillars, and partly by the Continuation of the Side-Walls of the *Temple*.

The *Posticum* of the *Temple* was equal to the Porch, having likewise a Gate, but all Temples had not *Posticums*, though almost every *Temple* had its *Pronaos*, or Porch.

The Middle of the *Temple*, called *Cella*, was a place inclosed with four Walls, having no Light but at the Gate, unless it were uncovered, as we shall shew hereafter.

The *Portico's* which make the Isles, were ranks of Pillars, sometimes single, sometimes double, which stood along the Sides of the *Temple* on the out-side: some *Temples* wanted this part.

The Gates of the *Temples* were different according to the difference of the Order of the Architecture, according to which the *Temple* was built: there was the *Dorick*, the *Ionick*, and the *Attick*.

The height of the *Dorick* Gate was taken by dividing into 3 parts and an half, the space which is from below to the bottom of the *Plat-fond* of the *Portico*, which *Platfond* was called *Lacunar*: they allow'd 2 to the height of the Gate under the *Lintel*: this height was divided into 12 parts; 5 and an half were taken for the breadth of the Gate below, for above it was straiter by a 3d. part. A 4th. part, and even an 8th. part of the *Chambranle* or *Door-Case*, according to the height of the Gate, which was to be less straitened above, the higher it was. The breadth of the *Chambranle* or *Door-Case*, was the 12th. part of the height of the Opening of the Gate.

The *Chambranle* or *Door-Case* grew straiter and straiter towards the top, *viz.* the 4th. part of its breadth: it was only edged with a *Cymatium*, with an *Astragal*.

Upon the *Cymatium* above the *Chambranle* or *Door-Case*, was a *Frise* called *Hyperthyron*, which had the same breadth with the *Chambranle* or *Door-Case*. Upon this *Frise* was placed a *Dorick Cymatium*, with a *Lesbian Astragal*; both of them jetting out very little.

Upon the *Moulures* the *Flat-Crown* was placed, with its little *Cymatium*, which jetted out the whole breadth above of the *Chambranle* or *Door-Case*, with its Mould.

The height of the *Ionick* Gates was taken as those of the *Dorick*; but to have the right breadth, they divided the height into 2 parts and an half: To allow them one and an half below, it was straitned at the top, as the *Dorick* Gate was; the breadth of the *Chambranle* was the 14th. part of the height of the Opening of the Gate; this breadth of the *Chambranle*, or *Door-Case*, being divided into 6, one was allowed for the *Cymatium*, the rest being divided into 12, 3 were allowed to the 1st. Face comprising its *Astragal*, 4 to the 2d. and 5 to the 3d.

The *Frise* which is called *Hyperthyron*, was made with the same Proportions that are in the *Dorick Order*. The *Consoles* or *Shouldering-Pieces*, descended directly to the bottom of the *Chambranle* or *Door-Case*, without comprizing the *Foliage* or *Leaf-work* that they had at the bottom: The breadth above was the 3d. part of that of the *Chambranle* or *Door-Case*, and at the bottom they grew straiter by a 4th. part.

The *Attick* were like the *Dorick*, but their *Chambranles* or *Door-Cases* had only a *Plat-band* under the *Cymatium*, and this *Plat-band* or *Face*, had only the breadth of 2 parts in 7, into which was divided all the rest of the *Chambranle* or *Door-Case* with its *Mouldings*.

Lib. 3. Chap. 3.

The Proportion of the *Temples* was so ordered, that they were twice as long as broad, but it is not to be understood precisely, but only of *Temples* that were without *Pillars*, whose length was divided into 8, and 4 were allowed for the breadth.

Lib. 4. Chap. 4.

Lib. 3. Chap. 3.

The *Temples* which had *Pillars* round about, could not have this double Proportion; for as much as the length had only the double of the intercolumniations, and by consequence a *Pillar* less than the double of the *Pillars* before and behind.

The *Aspect* of the *Temples* signifies two things in *Vitruvius*, *viz.* The Disposition of the parts of the *Temple*, in respect of one another, and the Disposition in respect of the Heavens.

As to what regards the Disposition of the *Temple* in respect of the Heavens, the Ancients always observed to turn them toward the Sun-rising, if the place were not ill-disposed for it, and that some great Street obliged them to turn it otherwise.

As to what belongs to the Disposition of the parts, *viz.* of the *Porch*, *Porticum*, *Isles* or *Oiles* within the *Temple* and the *Gates*, it was different in the *Temples* which were without *Pillars*, and in those which had *Pillars*.

Lib. 4. Chap. 4.

The *Temples* without *Pillars*, were those that were not 20 Foot broad, the length of these *Temples* being divided into 8, 4 were allowed for the breadth, 5 for the length of the *Temple* within, and 3 for the *Porch*.

Lib. 3. Chap. 1.

The *Temples* which had *Pillars* were of 8 sorts; The 1st. and the most Simple, was that which was called *Ad Antes*, because in this sort of *Temples*, there were only 2 *Pillars* in the Face or Front before, betwixt 2 *Antes*. There was 3 sorts of these *Temples*.

The First and the most Simple, had 2 *Pillars* before the Face of the *Temple*, at whose Corners there were 2 *Antes*, and the 2 *Pillars* supported a *Piedement* or *Fronton*.

The Second Sort had likewise but 2 *Pillars*, but they were between 2 *Antes* upon the same Line with the *Antes*; and these *Antes* with the 2 *Pillars*, made up the *Face* of the *Porch* of the *Temple*.

The Third Sort was, when betwixt 2 *Pillars* which were at the *Face* before, which made up the *Porch*, there were likewise 2 others within the *Porch*; these *Pillars* within, were not so thick as those without, although they were of an equal height; but to the end they might seem as thick as those without, they made more

Channellings, for the most part 28 or 32, supposing those without had 24; this was done to get more room within the *Porch*. These *Temples* had also this particular to themselves, that the Front of the *Porch* was closed with Partitions of *Marble* or *Joyner's-Work*, which ran from the *Ante* of one of the Corners to its neighbouring *Pillar*, and from this *Ante* to the other *Pillar*, and from this *Pillar* to the other *Ante*.

The second Sort of *Temples*, with *Pillars*, was called *Prostyle*; which differ'd not from the first, but in this, that besides the 2 *Pillars* of the *Temple*, *Ad Antes*, there were two others directly on the Angular *Antes*.

The Third Sort was called *Amphiprostyle*; because it had *Pillars* as well behind as before.

The Fourth Sort was the *Periptere*, which in the Front, as well as behind, had 6 *Pillars*, and 12 on every side, counting those of the Corners: the distance which was between the *Pillars* and the *Walls*, was equal to that which was between the *Pillars*.

The Fifth, the *Pseud-diptere*, viz. *False Diptere*, it had 8 *Pillars* in the *Front*, and as many behind, and 15 on every side, counting those of the Corners: the *Pillars* were distant from the Wall, the space of 2 Intercolumniations, and the thickness of a *Pillar*.

The Sixth Sort was the *Diptere*, which had 8 *Pillars* before and behind, and 2 rows round about.

The Seventh Sort was called *Hypethre*, because the inner part of the *Temple* was uncovered, it had 10 *Pillars* before and behind; and as to the rest, it was like the *Diptere*, but in this particular to it self, that all about it had two Orders of *Pillars*, at a little distance from the Wall, to make *Portico's*, as in the *Peristyles*.

The Eighth was called *Pseudo-Periptere*, or *False Periptere*; for the Disposition of the *Pillars* was equal to that of the *Pillars* of the *Periptere*: This *Temple* having 6 *Pillars* in the *Front*, and behind, and 11 in the *Isles* or *Wings*; but the Disposition of the Walls of the *Temple* was different in this, that they extended even to the *Pillars*, which made no *Portico*, for they were joyned to the Walls, except those of the *Porch* which were insulated, or stood alone like Islands.

The Round *Temples* were of 2 sorts; The first were called *Monopteres*, because they had no Walls, having only an *Isle* or *Wing*; viz. *Pillars* which supported a *Coupe*. Their Proportion was, that dividing the whole *Temple* into three, one part was allowed for the *Steps* upon which the *Pillars* were placed, which had their height equal to the distance that there was from one *Pillar*, to that which was Diametrically opposite to it.

The Second Sort which was called *Periptere*, had *Pillars* upon their *Basis* round about the *Temple*, the space that was between the *Basis* and the *Wall* was the 5th. part of the whole *Temple*, and the Diameter of the *Temple* within, was equal to the height of the *Pillar*.

The *Temples* after the *Tuscan* fashion were square, having 5 parts in length and 4 in breadth; the *Porch* which was as great as the rest of the *Temple*, had 4 *Pillars* in the *Front*; the Sides were closed half by the Continuation of the Walls of the *Temple*, half by 2 *Angular Pillars*; and there were likewise 2 *Pillars* in the middle of the

Porch: The *Temple* had 2 *Chappels* within on each Side.

We find that the Ancients had 14 Sorts of *Temples*, viz. 1. The Temple without *Pillars*. 2. The Temple *ad antes* Simply. 3. The Temple *ad Antes*, with 2 *Pillars* upon the same Line with the *Antes*. 4. The Temple *ad antes*, with *Pillars* of an unequal Magnitude. 5. The *Prostyle*. 6. The *Amphiprostyle*. 7. The *Periptere*. 8. The *Pseudo-diptere*. 9. The *Diptere*. 10. The *Hypethre*. 11. The *Pseudo-Periptere*. 12. The *Monoptere*. 13. The *Round Periptere*. 14. The *Tuscan*. See the Tab. 2, 3, 4.

ARTICLE III.

Of Publick Places, Basilica's, Theatres, Gates, Baths and Academies.

The Fabricks for publick Convenience were of six sorts, I. Market-places of the Greeks of the Romans, their Proportions; II. Basilica's, their Proportions, Columns, Galleries, and Chalcediques. III. Theatres composed of three parts; the Steps or Degrees which enclosed the Orchestra, the Scene which had three parts, the Pulpit, the Proscenium, and the Palascenium. And the Walking-places. IV. Gates, which were either natural or artificial, built three ways. V. Baths, consisting of many Chambers, their Description. VI. Academies composed of three parts, the Peristyle, the Xystile, and the Stadium.

Lib. 5. Chap. 1.

The Third Sort of *Publick Fabricks* are those which are Built for the Convenience and Use of all People; and there are Six Sorts of them, viz. *Market-Places*, *Basilica's*, *Theatres*, *Gates*, *Baths* and *Academies*.

The *Market-Places* among the *Greeks* were surrounded with Pillars close one against another. Among the *Romans*, the Pillars which environed the *Market-Places*, had larger Intercolumniations, for they made *Peristyles*, under which were Shops.

The Proportion of the *Market-Places* was so ordered, that having divided the length into three parts, they allowed two for the breadth; the *Basilica's* had never less breadth than the third part of their length, nor more than the half.

The Pillars were as high as the Isles or Wings were broad, and these Isles or Wings had a third part of the great Vault in the middle.

There was likewise a Second rank of Pillars upon the Wings, which made high Galleries, and these Second rank of Pillars were placed upon a *Pedestal* in the form of a Partition, high enough to hinder those that were in the high Galleries from being seen by those that were below.

At the End of every *Basilica*, there was a high and great Hall called *Chalcidiques*, which were joyned one to another by high Galleries: they served the Spectators while Justice was distributed.

The *Theaters* were composed of three parts, *viz.* The Steps or Degrees, which were instead of Seats for the Spectators: they were disposed in a Semi-circle, and they closed a void space in the middle and at the bottom of the whole *Theater*, which was called the *Orchestra.*

Lib. 5. Chap. 6.

The *Orchestra* was made in the *Græcian Theatre*, to Dance the Ballets. The Senators were placed in that of the *Romans*, because the Ballets were Danced upon the Scene.

Lib. 5. Chap. 6.

Lib. 5. Chap. 6.

Above and quite round the Steps or Degrees was a *Portico* of Pillars, the Steps being separated by divers *Palliers* or Landing and Resting places which went round, and by streight passages which went ascending from one *Palliere* or Landing place to another; so that the ways which led from the second *Palliere* to the third, parted betwixt those of the first, and ended betwixt those of the third. The Steps or Degrees were 14 or 15 Inches high, and from 28 to 30 broad.

Under the Degrees, above every *Palliere*, there were in the great *Theaters* 13 *Chambers*, in which were Vessels of Brass, set to several Tunes, or Tones; which by their Echo augmented the Voice of the Players. The Scene or Stage, was composed of the *Pulpit*, the *Proscenium* and the *Parascenium*. The *Pulpit* was the place where the Actors played: it was raised not above five Foot at the most above the *Orchestra*, or *Pit*.

The *Proscenium* was the Front of the Stage, which was adorned with Pillars of several sorts one above another. These Orders were so proportioned, that the second was a fourth part lesser than the first. The third diminishing according to the same Proportion.

The Front had three Gates, that in the middle which was the greatest was called the *Royal Gate*, the two others were called the *Gates of Strangers*.

Lib. 5.

These three Gates were closed with Machines, made in a Triangle, and composed of three Fronts or Faces well Painted, to represent Buildings in Perspective; they served for the changing of the Scenes, when these Machines were turned. And the Paintings represented three sorts of Buildings, which made three sorts of Scenes, *viz.* The *Tragick* by *Magnificent Pallaces*, the *Comick* by *Private Houses*, the *Satyrical* (*i. e.* the *Pastoral*) by *Fields* and *Groves*.

The *Parascenium* or *Postscenium* was the hinder part of the *Theater*, and the place whither the Actors retired and dressed themselves, and had their Rehearsals, and where the Machines were kept. Near the *Theaters*, were Publick Walks, in length a *Stadium*, which is about 90 *Perches*. There were Trees planted, and round about it were double *Porticos*, which were every one as broad as the Pillars on the out-side were high; for those within were higher by a fifth part, than those without, and they were likewise of a different *Order*; for those without were of the *Dorick Order*, and those within of the *Ionick* or *Corinthian*.

Lib. 5. Chap. 13.

The Ancients built their *Ports* in two manners; at those which were *Natural*, they only made *Portico's* round about with *Magazines* and *Towers* at the Ends, for to shut the *Port* with a Chain.

Those which were *Artificial*, were built three several ways: The first was to make Partitions of Wood only, without emptying the Water which was within the Partitions, and they cast into the Partitions, Stone and Mortar made with *Pozzolana*, thrown in hand over head; for they were certain that this Mortar wou'd grow dry in the bottom of the Water. The second Way was by making Partitions with ordinary Clay, or fat Earth at the bottom of the Sea, after the Water had been emptied out by Pumps. The third Way was to build a Mole upon the Sea-Coast, and to cast it in when the *Mason's* Work was sufficiently dry, which only required two Months time. That they might the better throw these Moles into the Sea, they built them half upon the Sea-Coast, and half upon an heap of Sand which they made close to the Sea-Coast; to the end, that this Sand which was stopped by nothing but by the Walls, built only to support it during the time that the Mole was a drying, might let it fall when the Sea came to carry away the Sand after that the Walls were beaten down.

Lib. 5. Chap. 10.

The *Bathes* of the Ancients consisted of many Chambers; some for Men, and some for Women.

Some of the Chambers had a moderate Heat, to warm their Bodies insensibly, and prepare them for a stronger Heat to make them Sweat.

The Chamber they were to Sweat in, was called *Laconicum*, and was round, and Vaulted like the ends of an Oven, pierced at the top with a round Opening, which was opened and shut with a Buckler of Brass, which hung at a Chain, by which means they augmented or diminished the Heat according to the Proportion that they pull'd up, or let down the Buckler.

One and the same Furnace heated both the Air and the Water, according to the Disposition of the places which were nearer or further from the Furnace, whose heat was communicated to the Chambers from under the Flooring, which was made full of little holes.

The Water was likewise diversly tempered by the different situation of three great Vessels of Brass, whose Water went from one into another, and there were Pipes that conveyed these three sorts of Water into the *Bath*.

The *Academies* of the Ancients, which they called *Palæstra*, was a place where the Youth learned Letters and their Exercises. They were composed of three parts, *viz.* Of a *Peristyle*, a *Xyste*, and a *Stadium*; the *Peristyle* was a Court surrounded with *Portico's*, which were of two sorts; three of them were Simple, and one Double.

The Simple stood in a row against three Bodies of Lodgings, composed of many great Halls, where the Philosophers had their Disputes and Conferences.

The Bodies of the Lodgings, which was the length of the double *Portico*, and one part of the Bodies of Lodgings which turned in, were distributed into several parts, for the Studies and Exercises of Youth; for there they had their *Classes*, their *Baths*, their *Stoves*, and their *Tenis-Court*.

The *Xyste* was a place planted with Trees, and surrounded with *Portico's* on every side: These *Portico's* were of two sorts.

There was one double which was set against the Bodies of the Lodgings, to which the double *Portico* of the *Peristyle* was joyned.

The *Simple Portico's* had two Wings, under these *Simple Portico's* there were hollow Ways, where they performed their Exercises; the rest of the *Portico* was raised to the right and the left, for those that had a mind to Walk while the rest performed their Exercises, in the hollow ways.

The Place which was compassed with these three *Portico's*, was planted with Trees, which made Allies, where the Wrestlers exercised in Winter, when it was fair Weather.

The *Stadium* was on the Side of the *Peristyle* and the *Xyste*. It was an Alley of 90 Perches; on each Side it had many Steps or Degrees, which made a sort of a long *Theater* bending in at both ends; these Steps or Degrees were made for the convenience of seeing them that Run.

CHAP. II.

OF PRIVATE BUILDINGS.

ARTICLE I.

Of the Courts of Houses.

The Courts of Houses were of five sorts, four whereof were made with jettings out, or Pent-houses of four sorts. the Tuscan, the Corinthian, the Tetra-style, the Vaulted, the fifth sort uncovered.

Lib. 6. Chap. 3.

The Houses of the Ancients had five sorts of Courts, of which the greatest part were covered round about by the Jettings which supported the Water-Channel or Gutter, in which all the Water that fell from the Roof met together.

These Courts made with Jettings, were of four sorts; The first was called the *Tuscan*, this Court was surrounded with a Jetting *en auvent*, which was laid upon four Beams, supported by other standing Beams placed in the Corners.

The second Sort was called *Corinthian*; it had likewise Beams, but they were further from the Walls than in the *Tuscan* Court, and they were laid upon Pillars.

The third Sort was called *Tetrastyle*, because the Beams were supported with four Pillars which were in the place of the standing Beams that were made use of in the *Tuscan Court*.

The fourth Sort was called the *Vaulted*; because the Jetting that it had round about, was supported by Vaults.

The fifth Sort of *Court* that had no Jetting, and which was called the *Uncovered*, had the *Water-Gutter* directly upon the Wall, and was only covered with the Entablature.

ARTICLE II.

Of the Vestibulum or Entry.

The proportion of the Vestibulum was taken three ways, for the length, breadth, and heighth. Of the Alley in the middle.

The Houses of the Ancients had *Great* and *Magnificent Entries*, they were sometimes 15 Perches long and 9 broad, and they were supported upon two ranks of Pillars, which made a Wing on each Side, the Proportion of their breadth and length was taken three Ways. The first was, when having divided the length into 5, 3 were allowed for the breadth. The second was, when having divided it into 3, 2 were allowed for the breadth. The third was, when having made an Equilateral Square, the Diagonal of this Square was taken for the length, and the Side for the breadth.

The height was equal to the length, taken from the Pavement below, to the bottom of the *Plat-Fonds* or *Flat-Roof,* which was hollowed on the other side the Beams, the seventh part of the whole height.

The Proportion that the *Alley* which was in the middle between the Pillars, had with the Wings, was different according to the Magnitude of the *Vestibule* or *Entry,* for the greater they were or the lesser, the Wings had a proportionable breadth with the *Alley* in the middle; So that if the *Vestibule* or *Entry* was 100 Foot long, the Wings had only for their breadth the 50th. part of the length; and when it was but 30 Foot long, they had only the 3d. part.

ARTICLE III.

Of Halls.

Three sorts of Halls, the Corinthian, the Ægyptian, and the Cyzican.

The Ancients had three Sorts of *Halls; Viz.* The *Corinthian,* the *Ægyptian,* and the *Cyzican.*

The *Corinthian* had Pillars round about against the Wall, and these Pillars supported the Floor made in form of a Vault. *Surbaissee.*

The *Ægyptian Halls* had their Pillars distant from the Wall in the manner of the *Peristyle,* and they supported only an *Architrave* without a *Frise* and without a *Cornice;* upon this *Architrave* there was another row of Pillars, between which were the Windows. The Floor which reached from the Pillars to the Wall, served for a *Terrasse* without.

Lib. 6. Chap. 6.

The *Cyzican Halls* had this in particular, that they were turned to the North, and had a Prospect of the Gardens; they were principally made use of by the *Greeks;* the Proportion of these *Halls* was as follows, Their length was double their breadth, and as to their height, this Rule was observed to have the height of all Sorts of Apartments that are not so broad as long, they added their length to their breadth, and took half of the sum for their height. The Apartments which were no longer than broad, had in height their breadth, and half their breadth.

ARTICLE IV.

Of the Distribution of the Apartments among the Ancients.

The Distribution of the Apartments different among the Greeks and Romans; what the Difference was.

Lib. 6. Chap. 10.

Lib. 6. Chap. 3, 4.

The *Romans* and the *Greeks* ordered and distributed differently their *Apartments*; for the *Romans* had their *Courts* and *Entries* magnificent: but the *Greeks* had only a narrow Entrance, through which they passed into a *Peristyle*; this *Entry* had of one Side a Porter's Lodge, on the other Side the Stables.

The *Apartments* of these two Nations differed in this, the *Apartments* of the Women were separate from the *Apartments* of the Men among the *Greeks*; insomuch that they Dined apart. They had likewise particular *Rooms* reserved for Strangers apart, where they only gave them Lodging, and never treated them above one Day.

CHAP. III.

OF THINGS THAT EQUALLY APPERTAIN TO PUB-LICK AND PRIVATE BUILDINGS.

ARTICLE I.

Of Aqueducts.

The manner the Ancients used to take the Level exactly. The Water was brought by Aqueducts, or by Pipes of Lead, or Potters Work.

Lib. 8 Chap. 6.

In Order to the bringing of Waters to Towns and Cities, the Level must be exactly taken; to the end, it may be known whether the Waters can be brought thither or no. The Ancients to this end made use of an Instrument called *Corobates*, which was directed by a Lead, and by Water, when the Wind hindered them from making use of the Lead.

They brought their Water three several ways; *viz.* by *Aqueducts*, by Pipes of Lead, and Pipes baked in a *Potter's* Furnace. They allowed for the *Channels* or *Sewers* of the *Aqueducts*, for every 100 Foot, half a Foot of Declination or Sloping; and if any Hills were in their way, they dug through them, making Vents to give Air at convenient Distances.

The Pipes of Lead were at least 9 Foot long; they made them of bended Sheets or Plates, and of different thicknesses, according to the Proportion of the greatness of the Pipes; these Pipes had likewise their necessary Declination or Sloping, and if any Valley was in the way, they made it equal to the Level with a Wall; they likewise made many Vents, to give the Water Air, and to know where to mend the Pipes.

The Pipes of *Potter's-Work,* were two Inches thick; they were joyned together with Mortar mixed with Oil, and when they had *Conde* or *Joynt* to make, they made use of a red Free Stone which they pierced through, to receive the two Ends of the Pipes.

ARTICLE II.

Of Wells and Cisterns.

The Precautions the Ancients used in digging their Wells, to discover bad Water, and in making their Cisterns.

It being remarkt oftentimes that the Water which is under the Earth hath many bad Qualities, and exhales vapours, which often stifles those which work in the *Wells*, after that they are dug, & the Water begins to gather together. The Ancients had this Precaution, to let a Lamp gently down into it, and if it extinguished it, they took it for an Infallible sign that the Water was bad.

The *Cisterns* were made to receive Rain Water in great Conservatories under Ground, whose Walls on all Sides, and at the bottom were built with Mortar of strong Lime, and Sand, and Pebbles, all well beaten together. They made several Conservatories, and the Water passed from one to another, to the end it might leave all the Dirt in the first and second; They likewise put Salt in their *Cistern-Water* to make it more subtile.

ARTICLE III.

Of Machines for carrying and lifting up great Stones and Burthens.

Machines for drawing Pillars, Architraves, for raising great Weights, three sorts; first, with a Handmill; second, with a Windlas, third, with several Ropes, to be drawn by Mens Hands.

Lib. 10. Chap. 6.

Ctesiphon and his Son *Metagenes*, Architects of the Temple of *Ephesus*, invented *Machines* to carry *great Stones*, out of which *Pillars* and *Architraves* were to be made. That which was made to draw the *Pillars*, was but a sort of a Frame as long as the *Pillars*, in the end of which were fastned Pins of Iron, which entred into the ends of the Frame, and served instead of an Axle-tree, the *Pillar* it self serving for a Wheel: And this had the desired Effect, because of the disposition of the place through which these *Stones* were to be drawn, which was a flat and level Country.

The other *Machine* for drawing of *Architraves*, was the same Frame which had two Wheels at each end, which supported the *Architrave*; which served instead of an Axle-tree.

Lib. 10. Chap. 2.

For the raising of great Weights, they had three sorts of *Machines*. The first was composed of three pieces of Wood, which were joyned together at top by a Pin which went through them all; so that there were two of these pieces which were on one side, a little distance one from the other, and the third was opposite to them; The two which were together on the one side, had a Hand-Mill which drew a Rope, which passed within a Truckle with three Pullies, of which that part which had the two Pullies was fastned to the top of the *Machine*, and that which had but one, was fastned to the VVeight to be drawn up.

Lib. 10. Chap. 2.

The second *Machine* was stronger than the first, because the *Moulin* had more Pullies, and instead of a *Moulin* or Hand-Mill, it had a great Wheel, whose Axle-tree drew a Rope which passed through these Pullies, and upon the Wheel there was another Rope twisted, which was drawn by a Wind-glass; sometimes the great Wheel was hollow, so that Men could walk within it, and so turn it.

The third had but one long and strong piece of Wood, which was kept up and stayed by Shrowds, as the Mast of a Ship is. By the help of these Shrowds, they bended and turned this piece of Wood where they pleased, drawing the Shrowds fast on the one side, and loosening them on the other. The *Moufl's* Crane as well those which were fastned to this piece of Wood, as those which were fastned to the Weight which was to be drawn up, had each of them three ranks of Pullies, which had three in every rank, that three Ropes might go through them, which were not drawn by Hand-Mills, nor by VVheels, but by Men who pulled several at one time at the same Rope: And that this might be done with the more ease, the three Ropes or Cables after having passed the last Pullies of that part of the *Moufle* which was at the top of the *Machine*; they descended down below, each upon one Pully, which vvas but the height of the Men: this *Machine* quickly povverfully lifted up the greatest VVeights.

ARTICLE IV.

Of Machines for Elevating of Waters.

Five sorts; I. The Tympan. II. A Wheel with Boxes. III. A Chain with Buckets. IV. The Vice of Archimedes. V. The Pomp of Cresibius.

Lib. 10.

These *Machines* were of four sorts.

The first was the *Tympan*, of which there were two sorts; The first elevated a great deal of Water, but not very high, for it only mounted to the Axle-tree of the *Tympan*, which was a great Wheel made of Planks which made two bottoms divided into eight from the Center to the Circumference, each Separation, having an opening half a Foot wide near the Circumference to draw the Water, which being elevated upon the Axle-tree, ran through the Cavities which were hollowed in each Separation.

The Second *Machine*, was a Wheel which elevated the Water as high as its Circumference, by the help of several Boxes which were fastned round about, and which poured out the Water into a Reeve as the Wheel, having mounted, began to descend.

Lib. 10. Chap. 2.

The Third *Machine* was a Chain with Buckets, as the one mounted, the other descended, being drawn by the Axle-tree.

The Fourth *Machine* was the Vice or *Skrew*, which is attributed to *Archimedes*, though *Vitruvius* makes no mention of the Inventor. This Vice was made of a piece of VVood, long sixteen times its Diameter: about this piece of Wood was put Obliquely a Hoop of Willow Hoop of Willow VVood besmeared with Pitch, and it was Conducted by turning from one end of the piece of the Wood to the other: Upon this Hoop others were put so that they were like the Vaulting of a Stair-Case whose ascent goes turning. This being done, this Vice was fastned and strengthned with Planks, which were pitched within, and covered with Iron Rings and Plates without: At the two ends of the piece of Wood, were Pins, which entring into the Suckets, made the *Machine* capable of Motion. This Vice or Skrew was placed according to the bent or sloping of the Triangle Rectangle of *Pythagoras*. This *Machine* elevated easily a great quantity of Water, but it could not carry it high.

Lib. 10. Chap. 2.

The Fifth *Machine*, was the Pump of *Ctesibius*; it was composed of two Bodies of Pumps, in which the Suckets having drawn the VVater when they were pulled up, they both pressed it violently into a Pipe which was fastned at the bottom of the Body of the Pump when they went down. For the VVater by the Impulsion of the Sucket, was forced to enter into these Pipes, because it could not go out by the Openings by which it entred, because of the Suckets which stopped them, these two Pipes were joyned together in a *Tambour*, which had likewise its Suckets, which hindred the VVater from descending into the Bodies of the Pumps, after it had been pressed into the *Tambour*, or *Vase*, which had another Pipe, through which the VVater was forced as high as they pleased, by Impulsion of the Suckets.

Lib. 10. Chap. 10.

All these *Machines* were either *moved* by Strength of Men, or by VVater-Mills, according to the convenience of the place.

ARTICLE V.

Of Water-Mills for Grinding of Corn.

The Water-mills of the Ancients were like ours.

Lib. 10. Chap. 10.

Water-Mills were moved by the help of a great VVheel which had many VVings, which were forced by the Current. The Axle-tree of this great VVheel, traversed another VVheel which had Cogs, which made the *Lanterne* or *Trundle-head* go, which was placed Horizontally, which was traversed by a Beam of Iron, which entred through above, into an Iron in form of a VVedge, which helped to fasten the Beam in the Mill-stone, above which was the Mill-Hopper, in form of a Funnel.

ARTICLE VI.

Of other Hydraulick Machines.

Three sorts of Water-Machines; first, for shewing the hour. Second, Organs.

Third, for measuring the Way by Water, by Land.

There were many other *Machines* which moved by the help of the VVater, as *Hour-Glasses*, *Organs*, *Machines* for Measuring the VVays, and knowing the swiftness or slowness of Sailing.

The *Hour-Glasses* marked the Hours by the help of VVater, which passing slowly, a little hole made at the bottom of a Vessel, and falling into another, in elevating it self insensibly in the Vessel which it filled, raised a piece of Cork, which hanging at one of the ends of a Chain wrapped about an Axle-tree, and which had at the other end a little Bag full of Sand, and a little lighter than the Cork: for this Chain turning, the Axle-tree likewise turned a Pin or Hand, which marked the Hours upon a Dial.

Lib. 10. Chap. 12.

The *Organs* played by help of two Suckets, which were pulled up or let down in the Bodies of the Pump. The Suckets pushed the Air with violence into a Funnel reversed in a Copper Coffer half full of VVater, and pressed the Water, and constrained it to ascend round about within the Coffer, which made that its weight in making it re-enter into the Funnel, pushed the Air into the Pipes, and made them Play, producing the same Effects that the Bellows did.

Lib. 10. Chap. 14.

They measured the way that the Ships make by the help of a little Mill, which was fastned to the Ship, and which turned by the resistance that its VVings found in the VVater when the Ship went forward and the Axle-tree of this Mill had a little Rong or Tooth, which every round pushed forwards one of the Teeth of the great VVheel, which turned another, and that another which turned a Pin or Handle, which marked the number of turnings, that the Mill made, by which means it was easie to take an account of the Perches, and Leagues that the Ship sailed.

They made use of the same *Machine* on the Land, fixing to the Nave of the VVheel of a Coach, a Tooth which made many VVheels be turned as in the above-mentioned *Machine*, at the last of which, was fastned a Pin or Handle, which marked the number of Perches and Leagues. This *Machine* had likewise a sort of a Counting VVheel, which at every Mile that the Coach went, let a Pibble fall into a Vessel of Brass, to give notice that they had gone a Mile.

ARTICLE VII.

Of Machines of War.

Three kinds; I. To dart Arrows, &c. II. To batter down Walls. III. To cover them in their Approaches to the Walls of the Besieged.

Lib. 10. Chap. 15.

The *Machines* of VVar of the Ancients were of three Sorts, for they were made either to Lance, Arrows, such as were the *Scorpions* or *Javelins*, such as were the *Catapulta's*, or Stones, such as were *Ballista's* or fiery Darts, such as were the *Pyroboli*, or they were made to beat down the VValls, such as were the battering Rams, and the *Terebra*, or to come covered to the VValls, and so safely Mount the Ramparts, such as were the *Tortoises* or *Testudo's*, and the Towers of VVood.

Lib. 10. Chap. 18.

The *Scorpions* were a sort of great Crossbows, which were made use of to defend the VValls, and which likewise the Assailants made use of in the wooden Towers, to annoy those that defended the VValls.

The *Catapulta*, lanced Javelins or Javelots, from 12 to 15 Foot in length, they were made of two Trees, set one against another, like the Masts of a Ship, which were bended in drawing them with a Hand-Mill. These Trees being on a suddain unbent, furiously struck together, and forced violently the Javelin. They were bent the one after the other by the same Cord, which was made of Guts, to the end, that the Master who managed the Engine, might be assured, that the two Trees or Beams were equally bent. He knew it by sounding the Cord when both the Beams were bent, and when the End above was drawn even to the Capital of the *Machine*, where they were stayed by a Pin of Iron, which was driven out by a quick stroke of a Hammer when they unbent it. There was a Cylinder which traversed an excentrical piece, by the help of which they heightned, or let down the End of one of the Beams below, according as the Master of the *Machine* judged it necessary, for the augmenting or diminishing their bent, which was known by the sound of the Cord, which was alike in both, when they were equally bent. See Table XI.

The *Ballista's* were bended and strung as the *Catapulta's*, but instead of Javelins, they cast great Stones.

Lib. 10. Chap. 22.

The *Pyroboli* were *Machines*, which lanced or cast Darts, to vvhich vvas fixed combustible Matter, vvhich was kindled vvhen they darted it against *Machines* of VVar or Shipping.

The Ram vvas to beat dovvn Walls and make breaches. It vvas a great Beam headed with Iron; it vvas hung by the middle, and pushed by the Soldiery vvith great violence against the Walls.

The *Terebra* vvas something like the Ram, being a strong Beam pointed vvith Iron, but it vvas sharp pointed, and it made vvay for the Ram, splitting the Stones.

Lib. 10. Chap. 20.

The *Testudo* or *Tortoise*, vvere great large and low Towers of Wood, which were rowled upon six or eight Wheels, they were covered with raw Hides to defend them from fire. Their use was to cover them that approached the Walls to undermine them, or beat them with the battering Ram.

The Towers of Wood were made to raise the Assailants as high as the Walls, to chace the Besieged away with Arrows and Scorpions, and to lay Bridges from the Towers to the Wall; they were sometimes Thirty Fathoms high, having Twenty Stages. They were covered, as the *Tortoises* with raw Hides; they had each of them a Hundred Men, which were employed as well to move them, as to annoy the Besieged.

FINIS.

ADVERTISEMENT.

The Figures inserted here are those only which are chiefly necessary to the understanding of Vitruvius, *that is to say, those which serve for the comprehending the Rules that Architecture gives for Buildings, now in use. The Figures of other things, of which* Vitruvius *treats, are omitted, it being enough to give One only, to serve as an Example of each kind, viz. one for all Temples, one for all Theatres, and one for all Machines.*

Plate I.

THE EXPLICATION OF THE TABLES.

THE EXPLICATION OF THE FIRST TABLE.

This Table contains the seven several sorts of Masonry; A is the first, which was called *Reticulatum*, because it was like the Mashes of Nets; BB is the second, it's called *Insertum*, that is to say, *bound Masonry*, because the Stones are one bound within another, every one being bound with four, two below, and two above: CC is the third sort, which was particular to the *Greeks*; it may be called double binding, for it's not only of Stones of the same course, but of two courses III. D is the fourth, called *Isodomum*, because the Beds or Lays are equal in height. E is the fifth, called *Pseudisodomum*, because they are of an equal heighth. FF, GG, H is the sixth, called *Emplecton*, because it was filled up any way in the middle. FF are the Stones which make the Courses. K is the seventh, which may be called *Compound*, because its Courses are of hewn Stone, and the middle filled up with Rubbish; and these Courses are fasten'd together with Cramp-irons.

This Table refers to *pag.* 18.

Plate II.

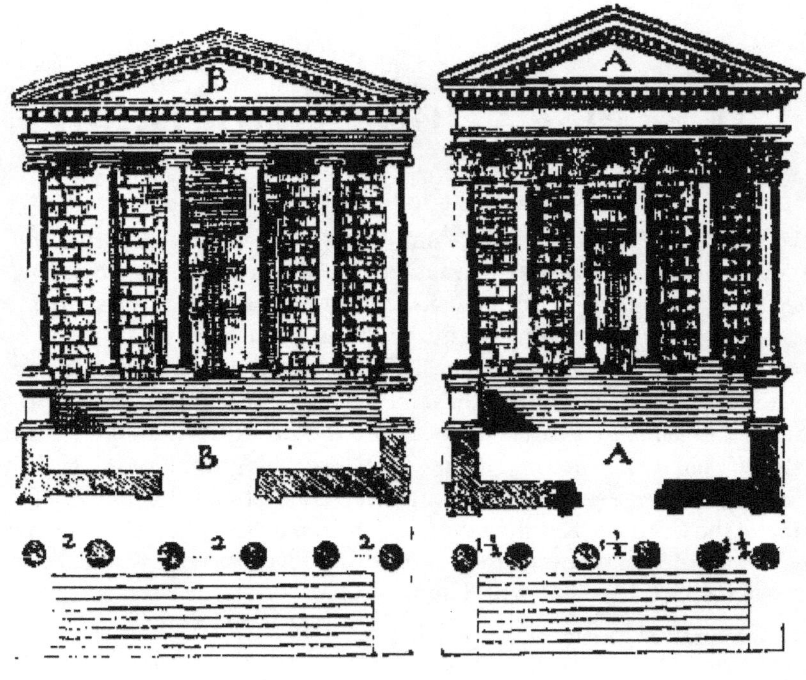
B
A
B
A

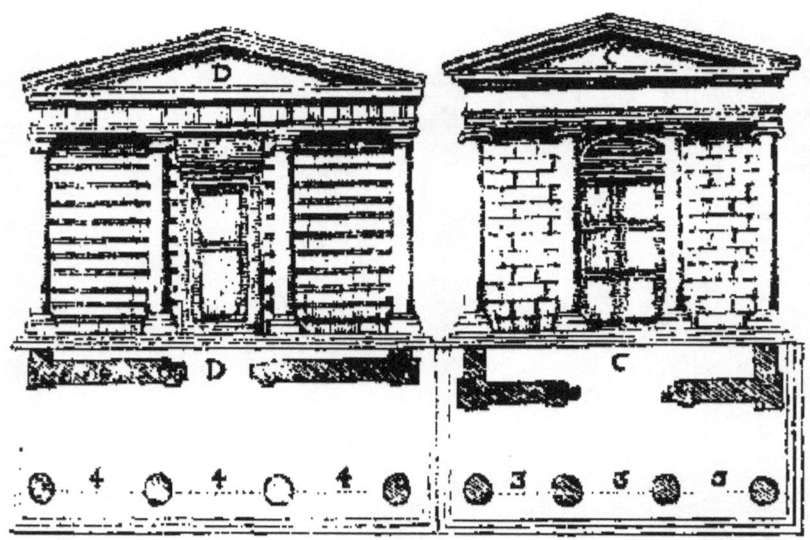
D
C
D
C

THE EXPLICATION OF THE SECOND TABLE.

This Table contains the five sorts of Edifices: AA is the *Pycnostyle*; that is to say, where the Pillars are very close, the Intercolumniation being but of one Diameter, and a half of the Column: BB is the *Systyle, viz.* where the Pillars have two Diameters of Intercolumniation: CC is the *Diastyle, viz.* where the Pillars are at that distance, that they have for the Intercolumniation three Diameters: DD is the *Areostyle*, where the Pillars are far asunder. There is no certain Proportion; we have given in this Figure four Diameters of Intercolumniation, it may have more: The fifth sort called *Eustyle*, is in the third Table.

This Table refers to *pag.* 31.

Plate III.

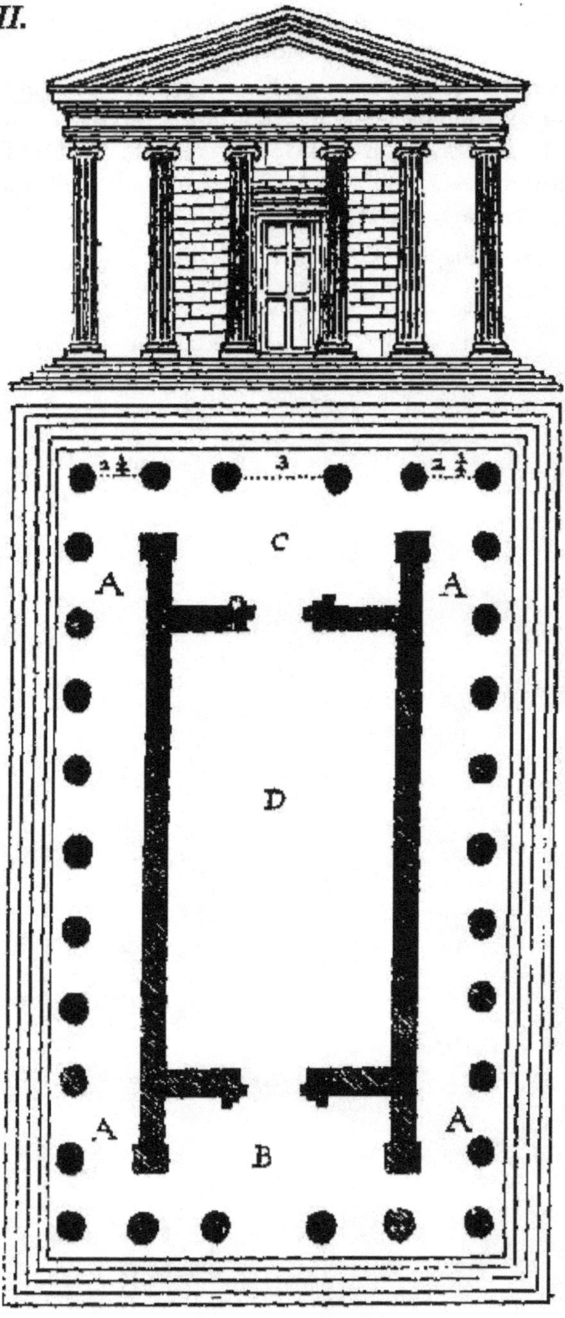

1¼
3
1¼
C
A
A
D
A
A
B

THE EXPLICATION OF THE THIRD TABLE.

This Table contains the Plan and Elevation of the fifth sort of Edifices, called *Eustyle, viz.* where the Pillars are distant one from another by more convenient Proportion: Its Intercolumniations have all two Diameters and a quarter, except the Intercolumniations in the middle of the *Face* before and behind, which have three Diameters.

This plan shews the different parts of the ancient Temples: AA, AA, are the Isles or Wings which are *Portico's*, having a rang of Pillars on the one side, and the Wall of the Temple on the other. B is the part called the *Pronaos* or Porch. C is the part called *Posticum, viz.* the hinder part of the Temple. D is that Part called *Cella*, or the Nave or Body of the Temple.

This Table relates to *p.* 31, & 45.

Plate IV.

THE EXPLICATION OF THE FOURTH TABLE.

This Table contains the Plan and perspective Elevation of a Temple, called *Hexastyle* and *Pseudodyptere, viz.* Which has six Columns in the *Faces,* before and behind, and which has simple *Portico's,* but which are as large as the two *Portico's* of the Temples which have them double. This Plan and this Elevation may serve for other Temples, which as to what concerns the essential parts explained in the precedent Table, are like to this here, as are the *Periptere,* the *Diptere,* and the *Hypethre,* which only differ in the number of Columns, or such-like circumstances.

Plate V.

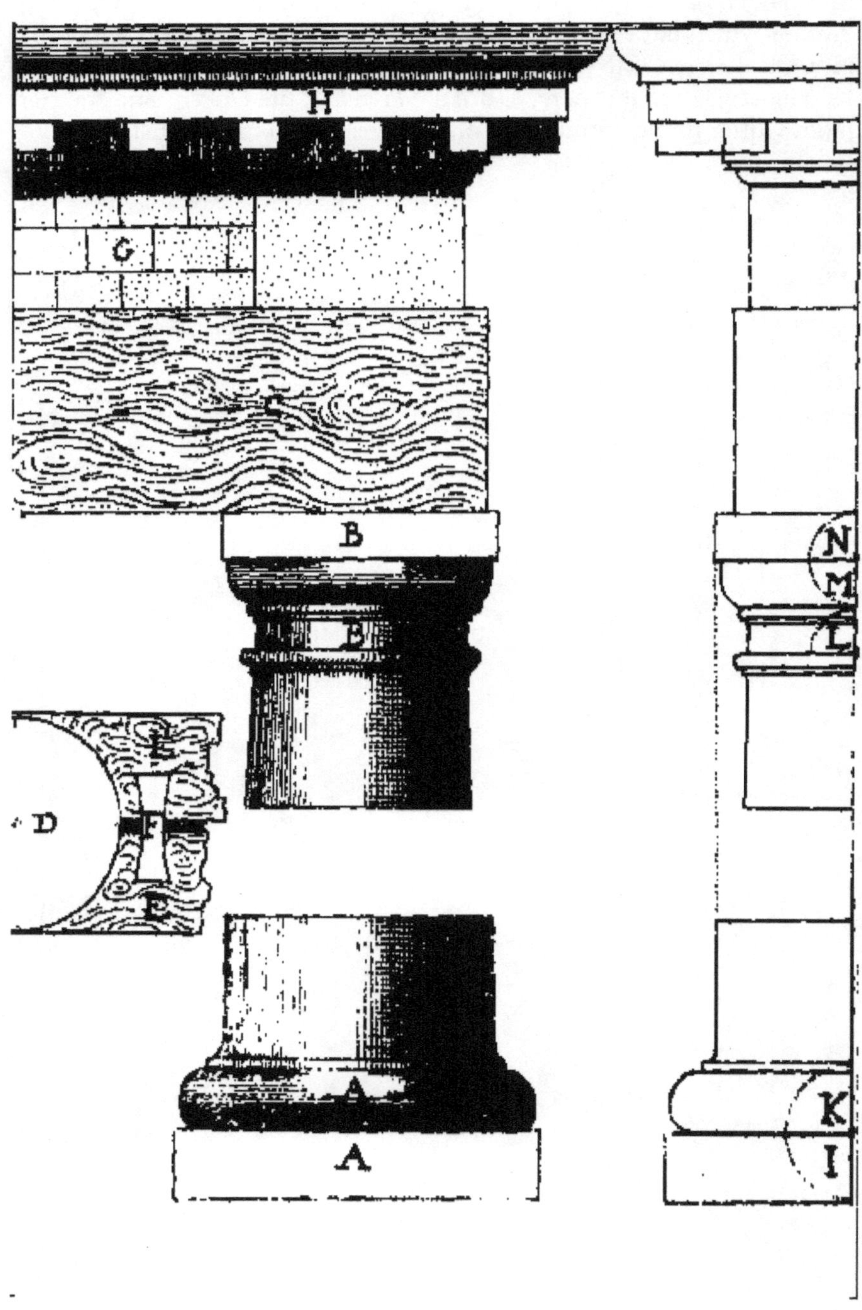

THE EXPLICATION OF THE FIFTH TABLE.

This contains the Proportions of the *Tuscan* Order. AA is the Base of the Column, which has for its height the first Semidiameter of the Column: It's divided into two equal parts; that below is for the Plinth, marked I; that above, marked K, is for the *Thorus*, and for the *Congè* or *Apophygis*. BB is the Capital, which height is equal to its Base: It's divided into three; the first marked L, is for the Gorge, with the Congè and the Astragal; the second, marked M, is for the *Echinus* or *quarter-round*; the third, marked N, is for the *Plinthus* or *Abacus*, called by the French *Tallor*. C is one of the *Faces* of the *Sabliers* which serve instead of an Architrave. EE is the under part of the *Sabliers*, which answers to the Diameter on the top of the Column, marked D. F is a Tenon shaped like a Swallows Tayl, which joyns the two *Sabliers* together. G is the little Wall which serves for a Frize. H is the Cornice.

This Table relates to *pag.* 36.

Plate VI.

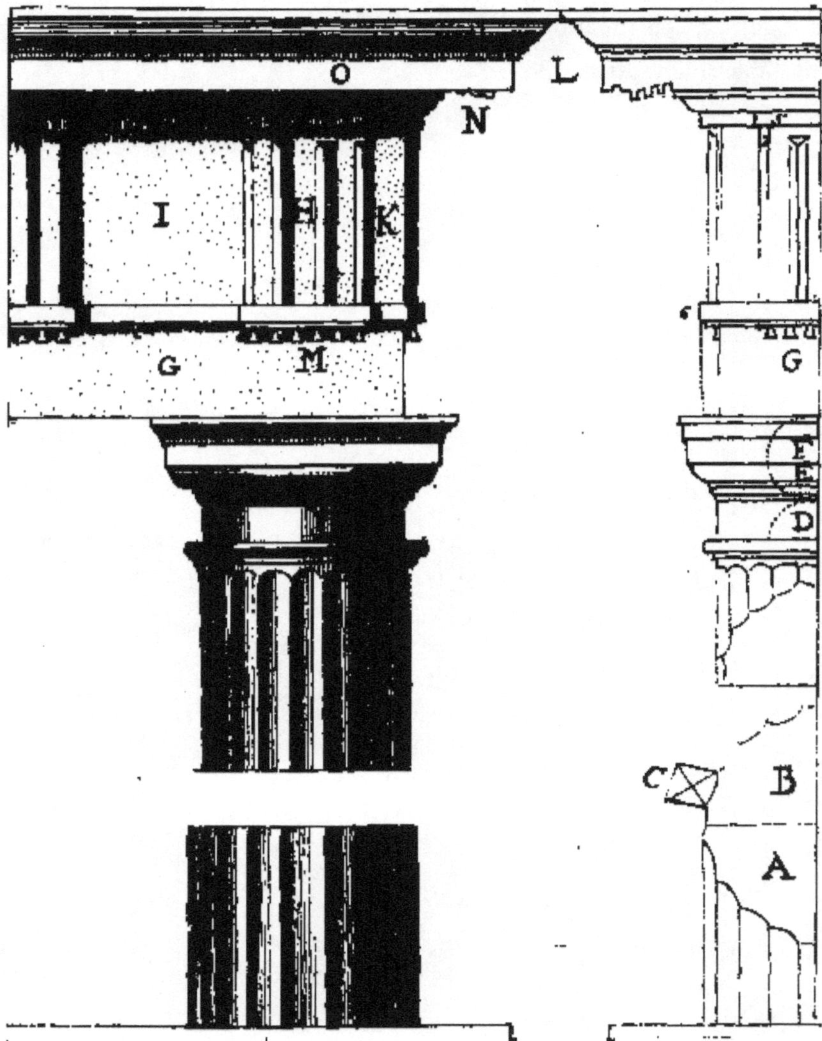
O
L
N
I
H
K
G
M
G
F
E
D
C
B
A

THE EXPLICATION OF THE SIXTH TABLE.

This contains the Proportion of the *Dorick* Order; AB is the top of the Shaft of the Column; this top shews the Plan of the two sorts of Channelling or Fluting, which are particular to the *Dorick* Order. The one half has Channelling or Fluting that is not hollowed, and make only *Flat Faces* or *Pans*. B is the other half, which has Channelings a little hollowed, *viz.* one quarter of the Circle: They are formed by the help of a Square C, whose sides are equal to every one of the Pans. D E F is the Capital divided into three equal parts. D is for the Gorge; E is for the Echinus, and for the Anulets or Rings; F is for the Abacus; G is the Architrave; H is the Triglyph; I is the Metop; K is the Demi-metop; L is the Cornice; M are the six pendant Drops which are under the Triglyph; N, O are the Pendant Drops which are in the Platfond of the Cornice.

This relates to *pag.* 37.

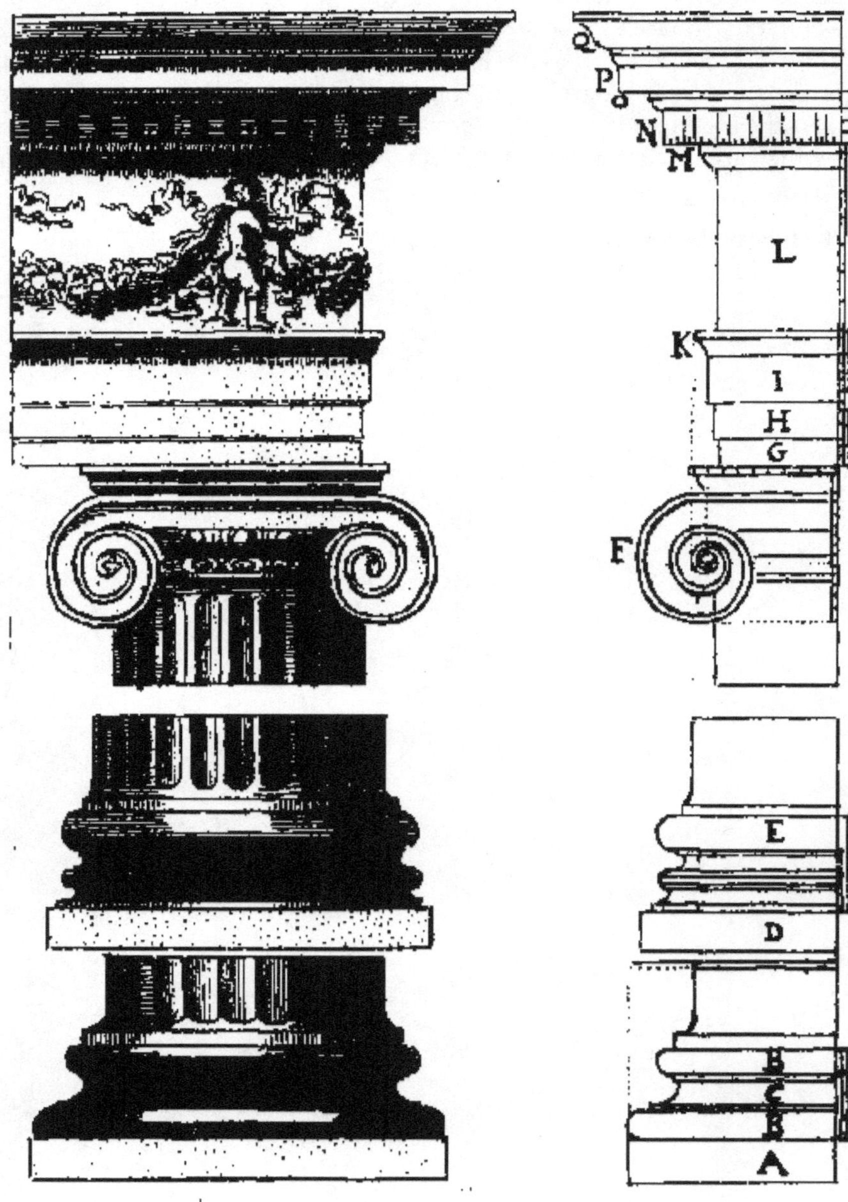
Q
P
O
N
M
L
K
I
H
G
F
E
D
B
C
A

THE EXPLICATION OF THE SEVENTH TABLE.

This contains the Proportions of the *Jonick* Order and the *Attick* Base: A is the Plinth of the *Attick* Base, which is the third part of the whole Base, of which the upper part is the fourth part of what remains after the Plinth is taken; the inferiour part is half of what remains, and the other half is the *Scotia*. C D is the Plinth of the Jonick Base, which is the third part of the height of the whole Base. E is the Thorus which contains three parts of seven, into which is divided what remains, the other four being for the two *Scotia's*, and the two Astragals, which are betwixt the Thorns and the Plinth. F is the Capital, whose Proportion is explained in the eighth Table. G, H, I, K is the Architrave, which has four parts, *viz.* the Face marked G; the second marked H; the third marked I, and the *Cymatium* or *Simaise*, marked K; L is the Frise. M, N, O, P, Q is the Cornice. M is the first *Cymatium*; N is the Dentil; O is the second *Cymatium*; P is the Crown with its little *Cymatium* or *Simaise*.

This Table relates to *pag.* 39.

Plate VIII

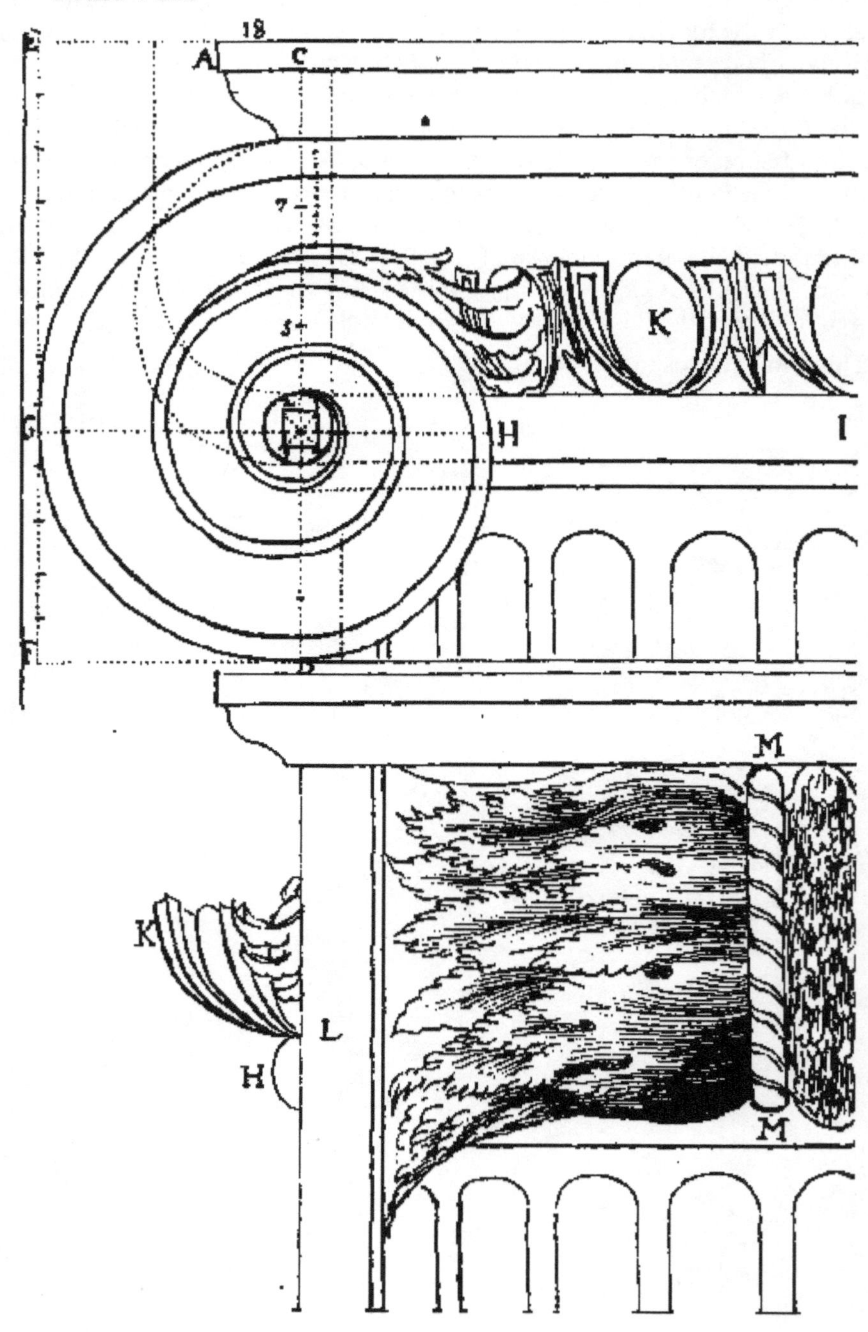
18
A
C
7
5
E
G
F
D
H
I
K
K
L
H
M
M

THE EXPLICATION OF THE EIGHTH TABLE.

This contains the Proportions of the Ionick Capital, of which only half is seen here: A B is the half of the breadth of the Abacus, which is regulated according to the breadth of the bottom of the Column, of which one half is marked B 18; for the bottom of the Column being divided into 18, 19 are allowed to the Abacus: A C is the *Retreat* which must be made of the Corner A, of the Abacus inwardly, to draw the Line C D, which must regulate the *Eye* of the *Volute* over which it must cross as it passes. To make this *Retreat* we must take one part and a half of twelve, into which is divided the height or thickness, E F, of the whole Capital, which height is equal to half the breadth of the Abacus. This height, marked C D, is divided into nine parts and a half, of which one and a half is given to the *Abacus*, and four and a half from the Abacus to the middle of the *Eye*, which is traversed by the line G H; the Figures 1, 2, 3, 4, mark the four Centers of the first four quarters of the Volute; the four second quarters, and the four third (for the Volutte has twelve) are taken in the Diagonal 1, 3, and 2, 4. H, I, is the Astragal at the top of the Pillar which answers the *Eye* of the Volute. K K is the Egg or *Echinus*; L is the Axis of the Volutes; M M is the ceinture of the lateral part of the Volutes. This relates to *pag.* 39-40.

Plate IX.

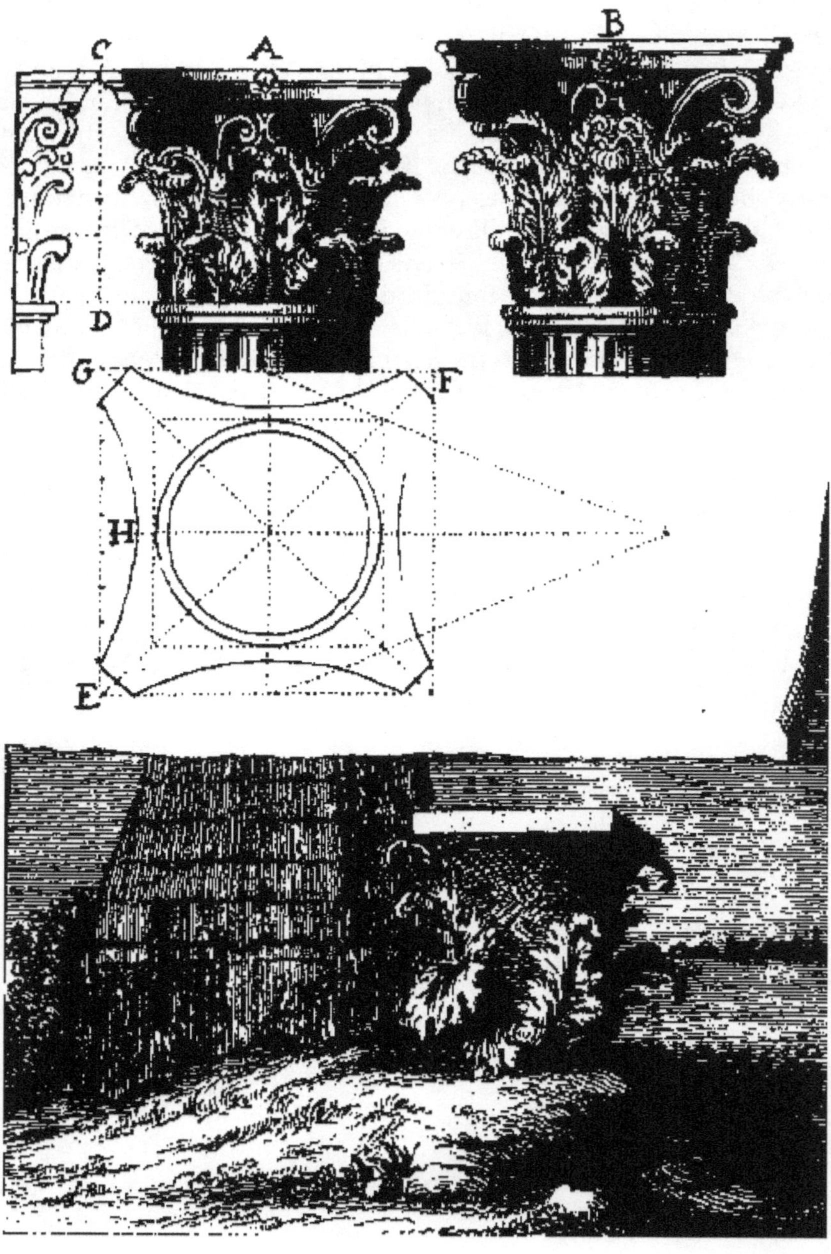
C
A
B
D
G
F
H
E

THE EXPLICATION OF THE NINTH TABLE.

This contains the Proportions of the *Corinthian* Capital, which makes all the distinction betwixt *Jonick* and the *Corinthian Order*, all other Members, according to *Vitruvius*, being the same. A is the *Corinthian* Capital, which has for its height only the Diameter of the bottom of the Column; B is the Capital of the Pantheon, which is higher by a seventh part, *viz.* the thickness of the Abacus; C D is the height of the Capital divided into seven, of which the Abacus has one, the Voluta's and Foliages and Stalks two, the Foliage in the Range above two, and that in the Range below two. To have the breadth of the Abacus, we must give to its Diagonal E F the double of its height C D. To have the greatness and just Proportion of its bending H, we must divide the breadth of the Abacus E G into nine parts, and give it one.

At the bottom of this Table is represented the Herb *Branbursine*, which grows round about the Basket, which is covered with a Tile, from which *Vitruvius* says the Sculptor *Callimachus* took the first Model of the *Corinthian* Capital.

This Table relates to *p.* 41.

Plate X.

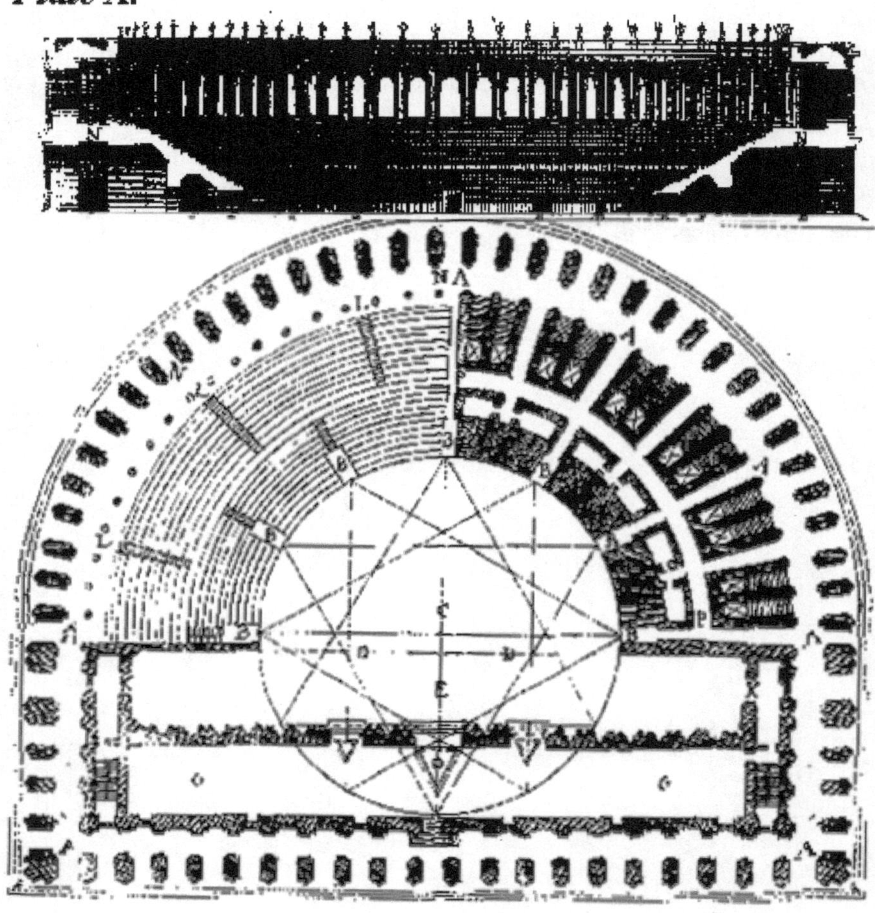

THE EXPLICATION OF THE TENTH TABLE.

This contains the Plan and Elevation of the Theatre of the *Romans*. AA is the Portico which went round the Theatre below. BB are the Entries through which they parted from the Portico's into the *Orchestra* C. KDEDK the Pulpitum or Stage; MM the landing-place which separated the Degrees above from those below: LM the Stairs which are between the degrees. NN the Portico above in the Theatre. PP the Passage under the degrees. TT the Stairs by which they mount to the Portico's above. KIHIK the Scene. H the royal Gate. II the Gates of Strangers. KK the Gates in returning. OOO the Machines used in changing the Scenes. GG the part of the Theatre behind.

This Table relates to *p.* 48.

Plate XI.

THE EXPLICATION OF THE ELEVENTH TABLE.

This contains the Explication of the Catapulta, which was a Machine of War used by the Ancients to dart Javelins of an extraordinary bigness. A are the two Beams one against the other, and joyn'd, which after having been drawn, pushed the Javelin with great force when they were unbent. There is one of these Beams, which is represented as being joyned to the Capital of the Machine by an Iron Pin, the other ready to be joyned when the Master of the Machine sounds the Cord with his right Hand, shall have it heightned or let down, the end marked C, as much as is necessary, to give it an equal Bent to the other. This is done by the help of an excentrical piece, which is traversed by a Cylinder, which the Master turns with a Laver, which he holds in his left Hand. D, E E is the Capital of the Catapulta. EE are the holes through which the Rope passeth to draw the Beams. F is the end of one of the Beams represented in great. G is one of the Pins which travers'd a round Eye, by the help of which the Beam is joyned to the Capital. H is the Cylinder which traverses the excentrical piece I. This Plate relates to *pag.* 60-61.

EXPLICATION OF THE HARDEST TERMS IN ARCHITECTURE.

A

Abacus, from ἄβαξ; which signifies a square Trencher: In French it's called *Talloir*; it's that quadrangular Piece commonly accompanied with a *Cymatium*, and serves instead of a *Drip* or *Corona* to the Capital. It supports the nether *Face* of the *Architrave* and whole *Trabeation*. In the *Corinthian* and the *Compound* Orders, its Corners are called the *Horns*, the intermediate *Sweep* and *Curvature*; the Arch, which has commonly a *Rose* carved in the middle.

Acroteria or *Acroter's* from ἀκρόν, *Summa pars*; they may be properly called *Pinnacles*, for *Pins* and *Battlements* were made sometimes more towring; but when they stood in *Ranges* with *Rails* and *Balisters*: Upon flat Building they still retained their Name, with this only difference, that such as were placed between the *Angular* Points, were stiled the *Median*, or middle *Acroteria*.

Annulets, are little square Parts turned round in the *Corinthian Capital*, under the *Quarter-Round*, called *Echinus*.

Ante, is a square Pillaster, which the Ancients placed at the corners of the Walls of the Temples.

Amphiprostyle from αμφὶ, *Circa*, and στύλος; *Columna* was a sort of a Temple which had four Columns in the Front of the Temple, and four in the Face behind.

Architrave, from a Mungril Compound of two Languages, αρχη *Principalis*, and *Trabs*; it's the first Member of that which we call *Entablature*; in Chimnies the *Architrave* is the *mantle*; over the *Jambs* of the Doors and Lintels of Windows, it's called the *Hyperthron*, from the Greek ὑπὲρ, *super* and θύρα, *Janua* or *Ostium*.

Astragal, from the Greek word αστράγαλος which signifies the *Vertebræ*, or little Joints in the Neck or Heel; hence the French call it *Talon*, or the Heel itself: It's a Member of *Architecture* joyned to *Bases*, *Cornices*, *Architraves*, &c. it's round like a Ring, and therefore it's called by the Italians *Tondino*.

Attiq; signifies after the manner of the City of *Athens*. In *Vitruvius* it's the Name of the *Basis* which the Moderns have given to the *Dorick* Pillar. We call *At-*

tiq; in our Buildings, a little Order placed upon another much greater; for instead of Pillars, this little Order has commonly nothing but Pillasters of a particular Fashion and Order, which we call *Attiq;*

Apophyges, vide *Congé.*

B

Basilica, from the Greek word Βασιλεῖς *Rex* or King among the Ancients. It was a great Hall which had two Ranges of Pillars, and had two Isles or Wings, upon which were Galleries: These Halls, which at first were made for the Palaces of Kings, were afterwards turned into Courts of Justice, and after that into Churches; which Form has always been observed.

Ballustre is the lateral part of the *Jonick* Capital. Our Workmen have given it that name, because it somewhat resembles a *Balluster.*

C

Chanel, in the *Ionick* Capital, is that part which is under the *Abacus,* and lies upon *Echinus* or Egg, and which has its *Contours* or Turnings on every side to make the Voluta's.

Cariatides are Statues of Women, which serve instead of Pillars.

Cincture is that part which makes the middle of the *Ballustre* of the *Ionick Voluta.*

Congé in French, in Latin *Apophyges,* from the Greek word αποφυγή because that part of the Pillar taking as it were a rise, seems to emerge and fly from the *Basis* like the *Proceltus* of a Bone in a mans Leg, In short, it's no more than the *Rings* or *Ferils* heretofore used at the Extremities of wooden Pillars, to preserve them from splitting, afterwards imitated in Stone-work.

Corona is properly that part of the Cornice which the French call *Larmer* or *Drip,* because it defends the rest of the Work from Wind and Weather: It is often taken by *Vitruvius* for all the Cornice.

Corona, called the *Plat* or *flat Crown,* is a particular Member in the *Dorick* Gate; it's made by so extraordinary enlargement of the *Face* of the *Corona* or *Drip,* that it has six times more Breadth than Projecture. This sort of *Corona* is no where found among the Ancients, but only in the Writings of *Vitruvius.*

Cymatium, from κυμάτον, which signifies a rouling *Wave;* is a Member of Architecture, of which the one half is *Convex* and the other *Concave,* the one being hollow above, and the other below. There are two sorts of them, the one called the *Gola* or *Throats,* or the *Doucine,* whose advanced part is *Concave;* and the other is called by the French the *Talon* or Heel, whose advanced part is hollow below, as the first is above.

D

*D*ie is the middle of the Pedestals, *viz.* that which is between their *Basis* and their *Cornice*. It's so called, because it's for the most part of a Cubit form, as *Die's* are that are used in play.

Dentils, or Teeth, is a Member of the *Jonick* Cornice, which is square, and cut out at convenient distances, which gives it the form of a Set or Gang of Teeth.

Diastyle, from διὰ and στύλος: *Columna* is a sort of Edifice where the Pillars are distanced one from another the breadth of 3 Diameters of the Pillar.

Diptere, from δὶς and πτέρον: *Ala* signifies that which has a double Isle or Wing; the Ancients called so the Temples, which were surrounded with two Ranges of Pillars, for there two *Ranges* made two *Portico's*, which they called *Wings*, we *Isles*, from the French word *Ailes*, which signifies *Wings*, because as Wings are on the sides of Birds, so these of Edifices.

E

*E*chinus, from ἀπὸ τοῦ ἐχίνου, a *Hedg-hog*; it is a Member of Architecture, which we call a *Quarter-round*; it has its name from the roughness of its Carving, resembling the prickly Rhind of the Chesnut, and not unlike the Hedg-hog; it's commonly next to the *Abacus*, and carved with Ovals and Darts, sometimes called Eggs and Anchors, because these pretended Chesnuts are cut in an Oval form.

Entablature signifies properly the Flooring or Lofting with Boards; it comes from the Latin word *Tabulatum*. In Architecture it's that part which is composed of the *Architrave*, *Frise*, and *Cornice*, for in effect this part is the extream part of the Flooring, which is supported by Pillars, or by a Wall if it have no Pillars.

Eye is the middle of the *Jonick* Volute, which is cut in the form of a little Rose.

Eurythmie, from εὖ *bene*, and αριθμὸς *numera*: it signifies Proportion; it's taken in its general signification in *Architecture*; for in its particular signification it signifies the true measure that is observed in Dancing after Musick.

Eustyle, from εὖ *bene*, and στύλος a *Pillar*; its the Order where Pillars are rightly placed, the Intercolumniations being two Diameters and a quarter.

F

*F*ace is a Member of Architecture, which has a great Breadth and a small Projecture; it's in *Architraves*.

Filet is a little square streight Member.

Fresco, and to paint in *Fresco* or *Freth*, is an Italian Phrase, and it signifies the Painting which is made upon the Plaistering before it be dry.

Frise is that part which is between the *Architrave* and the *Cornice*.

G

*G*nomonick is the Art of making Sun-dials; it's derived from the Greek γνώμων, which signifies that which shews a thing, as the Cock or Pin of the Dyal shews what a clock it is.

Gorge, or the *Gule* or *Neck*, is the narrowest part of the *Dorick Capital*, which is between the *Astragal*, above the Shaft of the Pillar and the Annulets.

Gutte, or *Drops*, are little parts, which to the number of six are put below every *Triglyph* in the *Architrave* of the *Dorick Order*.

H

*H*ydraulick, from the Greek ὕδωρ; which signifies Water, is an Engine that plays by the help of Water, especially where there are Pipes and Flutes.

Hypethre, from ὑπόσυὸ, and αιθὴρ æther; signifies a Building whose inside is exposed to the Rain and open Air. The Ancients called so all Temples that had no Roof.

Hyperthyron, for ὑπερ *super*, and θύρα *Janua*, a Gate or Door: It signifies that which is above the Gate; it's a large Table, which is upon the *Dorick* Gates in the manner of a *Frise*.

I

*I*chnographie, from ἵκνος *vestigium*, and γράφα *Scribo*, or *Insculpo*; which properly signifies the Figure that the Plane of the Foot impresses upon the Earth. By it in Architecture is understood that which is commonly called the *Plan* of the *Edifice*.

L

*L*acuner, or Platfond, is the *Flooring* or *Planching* above the *Portico's*.

Laconicum was a dry Stove to sweat in: It was so called, because it was much used by the *Lacedemonians*.

Larmier or *Drip*, vide *Corona*.

M

*M*etope, from μετι and ὀπὴ, *foramen*, *intervallum*. Signifies the Front; it's the Name of the empty spaces in *Freeze* of the *Dorick Order*, between the Triglyphs.

Modillion signifies in *Italian* a little Model, a little Measure: It's that part which is so often repeated in the *Corinthian* and *Compound Cornice*, which supports the Projecture of the *Larmier* or *Drip*. This part is called the little *Model* in respect of the great Model, which is the Diameter of the Pillar; for as the Proportion of an Edifice depends on the *Diameter* of the *Pillar*, so the greatness of the Modellians, their number, and their space or distances, must have a just Proportion or true Relation to the whole Fabrick.

Module or *Model* is a measure that is made use of to regulate all the Proportion of the *Fabrick*: In the *Dorick Order* it's half the *Diameter* of the Pillar; in other Orders the Module is the whole *Diameter*.

Monoptere, from μόνος *solus*, and πτὲρον *ala*; is that which has but one Wing or Isle; it was a sort of a round Temple, whose Roof was supported by Pillars only.

Mutuli, from μύτιλος, which signifies defect, as being made thinner, and more abated above than below. It's a sort of a Modellion in the Cornice of the *Dorick* Order.

N

*N*oyan is the middle part of the Flooring of the Ancients. They made it with Ciment, which they put betwixt a Lay or Bed of Pibbles, cimented with Mortar made of Lime and Sand.

O

*O*rchestra, from ὀρχὲομαι *salto*; signified the place where they danced; it was the lowest place in the Theatre, which was between the *scene, viz.* the place where the Players acted, and the Seats where the Spectators sate. It was in this place where the Greek Comedians were wont to dance.

Order, those Fabricks are said to be of different Orders, when the Proportion which is between the thickness of the *Pillars* and their height, with all other things which are required to this Proportion, are different.

Ornaments, *Vitruvius* so calls the *Architrave, Frise*, and *Cornice*.

Oval, vide *Echinus*.

P

*P*arascenium, from παρὰ and σκενὴ *tentonum*, is the back part of the Theatre or Scene.

Periptere, from περὶ *circum*, and πτὲρον *ala*, which has a Wing round about. This was a sort of a Temple, which had Pillars on all the four Parts, which was different from the *Prostyle*, which had only Pillars before, or In the *Front*, and from the *Amphiprostyle*, which had only Pillars before and behind, and none on the sides.

Peristyle, from περὶ *circum*, and στὺλος *columna*; signifies that which has Pillars round about: It differs from the *Periptere* in this, that the Pillars of the *Peristyle* are within, as it were round about a Court, and those of the *Periptere* are without, as in the Temples of the Ancients.

Pedestal, is that part which supports the Pillar.

Pied-droit is a square Pillar, which is in part within the Wall.

Pillaster is the same, with this Difference; that the Pillaster has a *Base* and a *Capital*, as a *Pillar* hath, which the *Pied-droit* has not.

Platt-band is a square Member, which terminates the *Architrave* of the *Dorick Order*, and passes immediately under the Triglyphs.

Plinthus signifies a Brick or square Tile. It's in Architecture taken for that square Member which makes the Foundation of the Base of the Pillar.

Posticum is the back Gate of a Fabrick.

Portico is a long place covered with a Floor or Flatfond, supported by Pillars.

Proscenium, from πϱὸ and σκενινὴ *tentorium*; it signifies the forepart of the Scene; it was an Edifice as high as the last Portico of the Theatre, whose Face or Front was adorned with many Ranges of Pillars.

Prostyle from πϱὸ and στὺλος, signifies that which has Pillars before only. This was one sort of the Temples of the Ancients.

Pseudodiptere, ψευδής *mendax*, δὶς *bis*, and πτὲϱον *ala*; signifies a *false Diptere*. This was a kind of a Temple among the Ancients, which had *Porticoes* round about, which were every one as large as the double *Portico* of the *Diptere*.

Pseudoperiptere, from ψευδής *mendax*, and πεϱὶ, and πτεϱòν *ala*, was a sort of a Temple, where the Side-Pillars were part in the Wall of the inner side of the Temple, which was enlarged sufficiently to enclose within the space which was allowed the Porticoes of the Periptere.

Pulpit was the place upon which the Comedians acted, which we now call the Stage.

Picnostyle, from πὺκνος *dentus*, and στὺλος *columna*; signifies a Building where the Pillars were very close one to another; so that the *Intercolumniation* had but a *Diameter* and a half of the Pillar.

R

Rudus was a sort of gross Mortar, which was made use of for smoothing, and equally filling and levelling the Superfices of the Walls, before the fine Plaister was laid on: It was likewise made use of for the second *Bed* or *Lay* of the Flooring.

S

Scene signifies a Tabernacle, Tent, or Pavillion, from the Greek σκενὴ. It was in the Theatre of the Ancients a great *Face* or Front of Building, adjoyned with Pillars and Statues, which had three great Openings, in which were Pictures in Perspective, which represented the Lodgings where the Tragedians and Comedians dwelt.

Sabliere is a piece of Wood as long as a Beam, but not so thick.

Scotia, from σκòτος *tenebræ*, *Darkness*, is a Member of Architecture, hollowed as a Demi-channel: It's particularly affected in the Bases where it's placed, between the Torus and the Astragals; it's sometimes put under the *Drip*, in the Cornice of the *Dorick* Order.

Statumen signifies generally whatsoever is made use of to support any thing in Architecture; it is Mortar mixt with Pibbles, which served for the first Lay or Bed in Flooring.

Systyle, from σὺν *con*, and στὺλος *columna*; signifies building where the Pillars seem to be joyned together, for the *Intercolumniation* is but of two Diameters of the Pillars.

T

Torus is a Member in the Base which is round, in the form of a great Ring; it comes from the Latin word *Torus*, which signifies a Bed.

Tringle is a little square Member, which is directly upon every *Triglyph*, under the Platt-band of the *Architrave*, from whence hang down the *Guttæ*, or pendant Drops in the *Dorick Order*.

Triglyph, from τρὶς *ter*, and γλὺφος *sculptura*; because it's divided into three parts, and engraved, it is a Member in the Freeze of the Dorick Order, directly upon every Pillar, and in certain spaces in the *Intercolumniations*.

Tympan signifies a Drum; it's that part of the bottom of the Frontons which answers the naked of the Freeze; it is triangular, and placed upon the Cornice of the Entablature, and covered over again with two other Cornices which slope a little.

V

Volute signifies wreathed, and turned about from *Volvendo*; it's a part of the Capitals of the *Ionick, Corinthian*, and *Compound Orders*, which represents the bark of a Tree twisted and turned into a Spiral line.

X

Xyste, from the Greek ζυτος, which signifies scraped; it was the place where the Wrestlers exercised; it was so called because they made their skins be scraped and rubbed smooth, to make the Sweat fall, and to make their Bodies more slippery, that their Adversaries might have the less hold of them when they closed.

Lector House believes that a society develops through a two-fold approach of continuous learning and adaptation, which is derived from the study of classic literary works spread across the historic timeline of literature records. Therefore, we aim at reviving, repairing and redeveloping all those inaccessible or damaged but historically as well as culturally important literature across subjects so that the future generations may have an opportunity to study and learn from past works to embark upon a journey of creating a better future.

This book is a result of an effort made by Lector House towards making a contribution to the preservation and repair of original ancient works which might hold historical significance to the approach of continuous learning across subjects.

HAPPY READING & LEARNING!

LECTOR HOUSE LLP
E-MAIL: lectorpublishing@gmail.com

www.ingramcontent.com/pod-product-compliance
Lightning Source LLC
LaVergne TN
LVHW091147180726
843490LV00004B/1352

9 789389 679625